1-95

KING ALFRED'S COLLEGE
WINCHESTER
Library: 01962 827306

To be returned on or before the day
marked below, subject to recall

other titles in the series

The Social Control of Drugs
PHILIP BEAN

Decisions in the Penal Process
A. KEITH BOTTOMLEY

Lawyers and their Public
C. M. CAMPBELL AND R. J. WILSON

The Factory Acts
W. G. CARSON AND B. MARTIN

The Politics of Abolition
THOMAS MATHIESEN

Social Needs and Legal Action
PAULINE MORRIS, RICHARD WHITE, PHILIP LEWIS

Knowledge and Opinion about Law
PODGORECKI, KAUPEN, VAN HOUTTE, VINKE, KUTCHINSKY

Deviance, Crime and Social Control
ROLAND ROBERTSON AND LAURIE TAYLOR

Pollution, Social Interest and the Law

NEIL GUNNINGHAM

Dept. of Law, University of Wales Institute of Science and
Technology

Law in Society Series
edited by
C. M. CAMPBELL, W. G. CARSON, P. N. P. WILES

Martin Robertson

First published in 1974 by Martin Robertson and Company Ltd., 17 Quick Street, London N1 8HL.

ISBN 0 85520 054 5 (paperback edition)
ISBN 0 85520 061 8 (case edition)

Printed in Great Britain by The Pitman Press, Bath

CONTENTS

ACKNOWLEDGEMENTS

I would like to acknowledge the very considerable help and support given to me by Ian Taylor of the Criminology Unit, Faculty of Law, University of Sheffield.

I also wish to thank Mike Russell of the University of Strathclyde, Dr R. A. Trevethick (Medical Officer, B.S.C. Rotherham), and Dr D. S. Oliver (Director of Research and Development, Pilkingtons Limited) for their assistance in providing material and information; Kit Carson and Zenon Bankowski, for their comments on the first draft, and Jan for typing it.

INTRODUCTORY NOTE

Among all the artefacts of social organisation, law is perhaps the one most prone to everyday interpretation as something independent of human fabrication. Born out of mundane purposes, disputes and aspirations—frequently lost in antiquity—legal proscriptions have a way of divorcing themselves from their profane social antecedents: they frequently become invested with a quality of moral authority either qua law itself, or as the assumed crystallisation of values which transcend sectional interests and temporal concerns.

For the sociology of law, the task of penetrating behind this autonomous facade is a vital one. In part, this may be accomplished by the accumulation of case-studies describing how specific laws have emerged as instruments for the pursuit of particular purposes. But this, in itself, is not enough, for a thoroughly sociological perspective on law is one which, among other things, attempts to generalise about the relationship between law-making and fundamental characteristics of the society in which it occurs. From this it follows that the case-study method is best pursued within a framework which is informed by broader theoretical perspectives on the nature of social order.

This link constitutes the organising theme in Neil Gunningham's analysis of law-making in relation to environmental pollution. Cast in terms of the debate between consensus and conflict views of society, this monograph attempts to show that the lack of effective legal control over atmospheric pollution in Britain cannot be explained within the framework provided by the consensus model of politics or by its pluralist variants. Instead, Gunningham argues, attempts to secure adequate legal safeguards in this area have frequently foundered because such controls are not in the interest of a dominant capitalist group wielding a disproportionate measure of political power. Even where such laws have been enacted, the author claims that they have either been so weak as to be virtually unenforceable, or have been systematically under-enforced by the relevant authorities. While such laws may serve to appease public opinion, Gunningham suggests that their capacity to impose effective and potentially damaging controls upon powerful interests is substantially neutralised.

While this argument is by no means beyond dispute, it is nonetheless an important one. From the sociological point of view, it focusses attention upon an area of behaviour which is not subject to clearly defined moral hostility, nor to stringent and consistently applied legal sanctions. It may well be that, as Vilhelm Aubert pointed out some years ago, such areas of societal ambiguity and legal ambivalence tell us more about the nature of our society than do the more familiar instances of uncompromising condemnation and remorseless legal control. For those who are more concerned with the issue as a vital area of contemporary public policy, Gunningham's argument may also be interesting for its timely scepticism about the extent to which the problems of the environment are amenable to legal solution, given the broader social context within which such solutions are likely to be devised and put into operation.

C.M.C.
W.G.C.
P.N.P.W.

INTRODUCTION

One of the tasks of a sociology of law is to explore the social
forces which bring about changes in the law. The present study
will do so by examining the emergence of criminal law relating
to atmospheric pollution, in an attempt to understand the
interests, processes and dynamics that have resulted in the present
formulation and administration of pollution control legislation
(and the lack of it) in Britain. It will also seek to compare the
forces which have resulted in legislation here with those which
exist in the same field in the United States.[1]

The study will consider not only the emergence of law but also
the reasons why some forms of polluting behaviour have not
been defined as crimes. This is to go beyond the examination of
crime legally defined and to recognise that no objective criteria
exist whereby to evaluate behaviour. To limit oneself to studying
that which is proscribed by the criminal law is to exercise a value
judgement for the legal, political and economic status quo, since
the definition of any activity as a crime (far from being objective) is always a persuasive definition embodying someone's ideas
of how people ought to behave and embodying special moral
claims.[2]

Since the definitions of crime and of social injury are prob-
lematic, since

> no scholar involved in the controversy about definitions of
> crime has been able to avoid direct or indirect use of moral
> standards in a solution to the problem[3]

we must openly face the moral issues. In doing so we should
recognise that unless law is based on consensus as to social injury,
then only one of a number of conflicting definitions of social
injury will be incorporated in the law.

9

To explain the emergence of criminal law relating to pollution then, we must have regard to the different definitions of social injury maintained by different factions of society, to their interests in having certain behaviour proscribed or protected by the law, to their relative power, and to the different means whereby these various groups may be able to impose their definitions in laws. As R. C. Akers recognises:

> we will have to scrutinise more carefully the process by which the criminal law is formed and enforced in a search for those variables which determine what of the total range of behaviour becomes prohibited and which of the total range of norms becomes part of the law

and we must also seek to isolate the factors operative in keeping certain behaviour *outside* the confines of the criminal law.

In studying the phenomenon of pollution, we are involved in what Wolfgang Friedmann describes as

> an area which until very recently has remained outside legal regulation altogether—a concomitant of the profit and consumer orientated society [but which] is likely to become a major object of social condemnation buttressed by criminal sanctions.[4]

However, although the United States has undergone a spate of pollution legislation, although it is in everybody's long term interests to control pollution, and although pollution represents an objective social problem now becoming subjectively recognised, comparatively little legislation has resulted in Britain.

Thus we are concerned with a particular kind of predominantly white collar, largely unlegislated, unapprehended, social problem, causing a considerable amount of social injury.[5] That the pollution issue affects a number of strong, political, legislative and economic interests raises questions as to whether the present legislative position is due to a tendency of criminal law, in societies such as our own, to favour the interests of certain economically and politically powerful groups at the cost of the less powerful, and as to whether law is unequally created as well as unequally enforced. So an explanation of the existence (or lack of existence) of legislation on pollution control may help to resolve vital questions about the nature of power in society, and

10

of the relationship between social structure and criminal law. If it does, pollution control becomes a fruitful area for study.

NOTES

1. The problems of pollution are inextricably bound up with those of increasing population and of diminishing natural resources, all of which can only be dealt with satisfactorily on an international basis. The present study is confined to the area of air pollution in Britain and America, but may serve to illustrate the politics of pollution control which may be of more general application.
2. "For sociologists of deviant behaviour and social problems, social values define their phenomena and colour their interpretations. All definitions and theories of deviation and social problems are normative. They define and explain behaviour from socially situated value positions". John Horton, 1966.
3. The Schwendingers, 1970.
4. Friedmann, W., 1972. Books quoted in the text are listed under the author's name in the bibliography.
5. For example Dr Percy Stock's investigations reveal that the incidence of lung cancer was strongly correlated with smoke density in the North of England and that cancer of the stomach and intestines was related significantly with smoke in the thirty County Boroughs investigated. More dramatically, over fifteen thousand people on Kyushu, one of Japan's main islands, have been affected by a massive outbreak of poisoning by polychlorinated biphenyls—only recently under voluntary ban in Britain. *The Guardian*, 25.9.72.

Chapter One: THEORIES OF LAW CREATION

To understand the present state of pollution control legislation we need to consider how the history and evolution of laws have been treated by sociologists. Those whose views seem most relevant to the issue of pollution legislation will be particularly examined. In later chapters we will discuss, by reference to such theories, if, when, how and why environmental legislation is created.

Theories couched in general terms about the creation of rules, concern "whose values are, and whose values ought to be, embodied in the law and whose conception of what society ought to be like determines the legal structure of the State".[1]

Two answers have been offered, embodying the order and conflict models of society. The order model stresses the cohesion, solidarity, integration, co-operation and stability of society, which is seen as united by shared culture, and by agreement on the norms and values that underpin it. Although order theory does not necessarily deny *some* disagreement, it is viewed as resolved by mutually agreed processes. Power represents legitimate authority, upholding commonly held beliefs and sentiments.

The conflict model sees society as an unstable system involving a continuous political struggle between conflicting hostile groups with different goals and values. The maintenance of power requires inducement and coercion, and law is an instrument of repression perpetuating the interests of the powerful at the cost of alternative interests, norms and values.

The Order View

The order view in classical social theory stems from the work of

13

Durkheim, particularly his analysis of types of law in relation to types of social solidarity. For Durkheim, juridicial rules could be classified into two types according to the different sanctions which they imposed. The one (repressive law) involves penal sanctions, the other (restitutive law) involves only the "re-establishment of troubled relations to their normal state" by means of civil law.

These two types of law correspond to two types of social solidarity—mechanical and organic. The former occurs in primitive, unsophisticated societies in which there is little separation of social functions. Under such conditions individuality is subordinated to the pressure of the collective conscience, and the law, repressive of individuality, represents the elements of social life which the common conscience embraces and regulates.

In Durkheim's description of repressive law, the order vocabulary is clear. Society is regarded as one unified whole, with a common culture, a collective conscience, agreed values and aims and consensus on the content of the criminal law. He states that

> in effect, the only common characteristic of all crimes is that they consist in acts universally disapproved of by members of each society . . . that crime shocks sentiments which, for a given social system are found in all healthy consciences.

Durkheim goes on to contrast law in modern societies which are characterised by the division of labour. He describes the emergence of restitutive law which testifies to the collapse of the hold of the collective conscience and

> to the growth of individuality of interest, function and identity encouraged and developed by the specialisation of task in the division of labour. Under these conditions of organic solidarity, the tension between the interests of the conscience collective and those of men with individual interests . . . is opened up.[2]

But although Durkheim recognises the co-existence and conflict of different sets of values and interests under a forced division of labour, he does not regard conflict as endemic in society. That he regards society rather as a natural system based on consensus is clear from the organic model he employs in analysis. Conflict is caused essentially by some pathology within the organism of society which causes system imbalance. This can be rectified and a healthy (consensual) society restored by the development of

14

the 'spontaneous' rather than the 'forced' division of labour.[3]

Various other versions of order theory, assuming consensus, have emerged from the work of legal philosophers. For example, it has been recognised that natural law theories

> presuppose that the choice of values embodied in the law derives from a source equally authoritative for all mankind [and] assume that this set of authoritative values is appropriate for determining what law ought to be.[4]

They thus deny that there can be any significant conflict between different interest groups because if dispute can be resolved by appeal to a single authoritative standard, the arbiter need not make a value choice. But the standard appealed to and identified with eternal truth is always custom or "the intuitive apprehensions of truth which invariably reflect the subjective values of the author",[5] and the existence of a monolithic set of values has yet to be demonstrated. Natural law theories further flounder in the absence of public consensus as to what specific policies or procedures will maximise justice and legality and they fail to account for the cultural and temporal relativity of law.

A number of models, realising the deficiencies of natural law, have acknowledged the value choice of lawmakers, but some of these are no more satisfactory. For example positivism, in the form it took under Austin, treated law "as an isolated block of concepts that have no relevant characteristics or functions apart from their possible validity or invalidity within a hypothetical system",[6] and served "to suggest a framework for viewing law as a logically self-consistent system . . . not to provide a theory of how power was, or ought to be, distributed in society".[7] As Schur has noted, such formalistic approaches, with their concern for the function of legal consistency, can never embrace the reality of law as a living institution that can only be described and understood by systematically studying what is taking place at all stages of the legal process, from the making of laws to the release of law violators. This insight of the Legal Realists has made it apparent that the legal system has an inevitable flexibility, and that new laws are passed in an effort to solve perceived problems of prevailing social conditions.

However, this explains neither why something is perceived as a problem, nor in what circumstances such a perception results in

15

legislation. Neither does it specifically explain how changes in the legal order come about. Still retaining the order/conflict dichotomy, two competing general hypotheses have been offered— the 'value expression' and 'interest group' hypotheses.

In the order perspective the criminal law

> represents a sustained effort to preserve important social values from serious harm and to do so not arbitrarily but in accordance with rational methods directed toward the discovery of past ends.[8]

Legal norms are seen

> as an expression of those societal values which transcend the immediate interests of individuals or groups [and] as emerging through the dynamics of cultural processes as a solution to certain needs and requirements which are essential for maintaining the fabric of society.[9]

P. A. Sorokin thus emphasises the logical connection between the laws and the dominant values of the culture, and for him, men who make the rules become the instruments through which the culture mentality expresses itself in specific legal rules.

We have noted that Durkheim also saw law as an expression of the common consciousness or spirit of the people. Critics, however, have questioned whether there actually is such a common or public consciousness, and if so, how important it is in shaping law. They point to the many instances where specific interests can be shown to have moulded the law; perhaps proponents of this order perspective, as A. K. Cohen suggests, must retreat to a position whereby they claim that only the general character of the body of the laws in existence at any time reflects the values of the period, without requiring that every single law does so to the same degree.

But even if value expression theories represent an inadequate scheme for explaining the development of law, their exponents emphasise "that ways of viewing law in general, as well as the specific content of substantive law, undoubtedly are associated with and reflect broader societal value orientations".[10] Thus Friedmann claims that, although the power of those who control the machinery of the State has been enormously increased by the development of the modern legislative and administrative machinery, as well as by the growing concentration of physical

16

and technical power and the means of communication, nevertheless there is always some inter-relation between the State machinery which produces the changes, and the social opinion of the community in which they are intended to operate. The kind of inter-relation that obtains in any given situation is essentially determined by the type of political system that controls legal action, and the type of social interest which is the object of the legal regulation in question.

In a democracy, public opinion on vital social issues constantly expresses itself, not only through public discussion in the press, radio, pressure groups, but through scientific and professional associations.[11]

But Friedmann fails to acknowledge that there may be no consensus on what is to be regarded as a vital social issue or on how it is to be resolved. Moreover, what becomes a vital social issue depends upon it becoming a subjective social problem and this in turn, it will be shown, depends largely upon the abilities of various moral entrepreneurs or vested interests to impose their definitions on the situation.

Such criticisms can still be resolved within an order model if the State itself is viewed as providing a value-neutral framework within which the struggle of competing but balanced interests is contained. Instead of assuming that society has a set of shared values, this perspective acknowledges that there is a plurality of of norms and values, and that the population is heterogeneous, but, underlying the disagreement of competing interests it sees a consensus on how conflict is to be resolved. The legislature is thus an arena within which disputes are resolved by groups reflecting the power configurations of society. Although it is not itself value-neutral, it operates as a consequence of the framework of elections, which is value-neutral. No group can become a ruling class or power elite (whose control over the instruments of power enables it to oppress its opponents) because power is scattered among a number of groups or co-ordinated associations, none of which is dominant. Those who occupy positions of power are checkmated either by other groups, by the electorate or by constitutional codes.

The concept of occupational or co-ordinated associations is often central to such pluralist models of society. Durkheim, for

17

example, saw the formation of occupational associations as one of the factors necessary to produce a system of laws expressing the social needs of society. Neither the State nor a political society could do this because the specialized nature of economic life escapes their control and understanding. An occupational association, on the other hand, is intimate enough with economic life to know its functioning, feel its needs, and able to follow its variations. Society, he writes, instead of remaining an aggregate of juxtaposed territorial districts

> would become a vast system of natural corporations . . . in this way political assemblies would more exactly express the diversity of social interests and their relations. They would be a more faithful picture of social life in its entirety.

However, the pluralistic model has been severely criticised, particularly by C. Wright Mills, who argues that there is no equality of power because some associations are more powerful than others; by virtue of being at the centre of power, these are more able to reinforce their interests than those at the periphery. Further, the majority are often apathetic or unaware of an issue, but even when they are concerned they are frequently unable to organise and thus successfully impose their opinion on the legislature.[12] Even those who are members of a significant co-ordinated association are not necessarily enabled thereby to develop any coherent structural view of the political process.

> Thus the assumption implicit in pluralistic theory that the differentiation of social life and organization facilitates the playing off of interest in a fluent and egalitarian fashion—is not an assumption borne out by the facts of institutional order.[13]

Pluralistic theory has been further attacked by Chambliss and Seidman who contend that

> far from being primarily a value-neutral framework within which conflict can be peacefully resolved, the power of the State is itself the principal prize in the perpetual conflict that is society. . . . In a society sharply divided into haves and have nots . . . powerful and weak, shot with a myriad of special interest groups, not only is the myth false because of imperfections in the normative system: It is *inevitable* that it be so. . . . Whosoever is in control of the State uses it in his own interest. Since his own interest requires the exclusion of his

antagonists from participation in decision making, even the processes by which the struggle for state power is carried on are warped in favour of one contending group or another.

They reject the value-free model of the State because the activities of the government are not confined merely to the application of fixed rules to facts, but in large part consist in the exercise of discretion in creating (or not creating) rules. Such rules are normative and, as such, are value-laden. They are achieved by a process of bargaining, but the success of the various parties to that bargaining depends greatly on the rules of the game within Congress.[14] The constitution itself cannot be value-free. Moreover, the very nature of the governmental framework requires that there be certain costs involved in contesting issues of law and those better able to afford the invocation of governmental processes will inevitably be in an advantageous position. The relative costliness of governmental processes is itself a value-ladened issue.

These criticisms serve to refute Friedmann's claim that

> because of the constant interaction between the articulation of public opinion and the legislative process, the tension between the legal and the social norm can never be too great. It is not possible to impose a law on an utterly hostile community.

Friedmann is never able to demonstrate the existence of any constant interaction between public opinion and legislation. In as much as his view is based on consensus reflected in abstract value-agreement with legislative action on the part of the population, he is in danger of ignoring the gap which may exist between expressed attitudes and actual action. Belief informed may not be belief determined, and advocates of the order perspective are open to accusations of making unsubstantiated assumptions about an unresolved problem of social theory.

An Alternative Perspective: Conflict Theory

Conflict theories, reacting against the utilitarian view that law reflects public opinion, can establish a surer factual basis for their concept of law as an instrument of social control in the

19

hands of powerful interest groups, and they can point to various studies which confirm their general orientation.

Chambliss has reviewed a number of studies in which the role of interest groups in determining the content of legal norms is paramount. Thus both Hall's analysis of the emergence of laws on theft, and that of Chambliss of the shifts and alterations of the vagrancy statutes, revealed interest groups of sufficient power to influence legislation. In the latter case these laws were a legislative innovation which reflected the socially perceived necessity of providing an abundance of cheap labour for land-owners during a period when serfdom was breaking down and when the pool of available labour was depleted. The findings are in agreement with Weber's contention that 'status groups' determine the content of the law, but they are inconsistent with the perception of law as a reflection of public opinion.

This does not mean that the former analysis will always necessarily be correct but Chambliss is led to conclude that "these analyses of the emergence of criminal laws, then, suggest that many and perhaps most of the laws emerge through the efforts of vested-interest groups".[15]

Nevertheless he acknowledges that not all laws represent the interests of persons in power at the expense of the less influential—some laws represent consensus while others reflect the interests of the general population and are antithetical to those in power. He concludes "the influence of interest groups, then, is but one aspect of the processes which determine the emergence and focus of the legal norms".

Other contemporary theorists have reached similar conclusions:

> though conceding in various degrees the existence of some legislation reflecting consensus or interests transcending the particularistic concerns of identifiable interest groups, on balance their emphasis is upon criminal law as mirroring diversity of interests, shifting distributions of power, and the maintenance of social order through use of the State's most efficient apparatus of coercion.[16]

W. G. Carson (1971) has defended this conflict/power model of the criminal law against various objections by pointing out that, despite the existence of criminal legislation placing proscriptions on the behaviour of groups in positions of power, these may be infrequently enforced or "the barriers to the efficient implementation of such laws may be built in at the legislative stage itself". He gives examples of statutes which overtly constrain the powerful but which are not, in fact, all that antithetical to their interests, and of "compromise bills to lessen the dissatisfaction of multiple interest groups". He states his own view that the emergence of criminal law in complex societies is not merely a function of the exercise of power by a homogenous power elite but is a process "in which many powerful groups compete and—from time to time—coalesce, giving rise to legislation frequently distinguished by compromise rather than by outright victory". However, he does not deny that substantial consensus also exists over a range of criminal laws at any stage in time.

More extreme is Chambliss and Seidman's conception of society as constantly in strife, and of

> the State and its vast machinery for creating myth and symbol, for inspiring support even from those whose interests are most injured by its activity, and in the final analysis, its monopoly of the means of violence and coercion, [of] itself at once the principal weapon and main prize in the struggle.[17]

From the foregoing it can be seen that conflict theorists, whilst united in emphasising that interest, power and coercion are essential to an understanding of society, show no unanimity in their analysis of the basis of power and interest. Yet it is essential to examine the basis of conflict since we must have a concept of who holds power in what sort of structure, and to what ends, in order to understand and predict the outcome of social conflict, and the kinds of social norms, interests and goals that will have the protection of the law.

It is particularly important to distinguish the positions of Marx and Weber.[18] Marx believed that all non-primitive societies could be divided fundamentally into two classes of people—ruling and subject classes—between whom there is a perpetual struggle. The nature and course of this conflict is primarily influenced by the development of productive forces, dominance being maintained by the possession in the hands of the ruling class of the major instruments of economic production. Under capitalism the conflict is sharpest because of the widening gulf between rich and poor.

Weber, in contrast, saw society as stratified both by social class and by social prestige or honour, and maintained that political power is an independent phenomenon. He also believed that the capitalist class was itself divided—between financial capitalists and industrialists and by conflict between different branches of industry competing with each other over the distribution of scarce resources in a market situation.

Contemporary conflict theory has been influenced by Dahrendorf, who argues that in 'post-capitalist society' the coincidence of economic and political conflict, basic to Marx, has ceased to exist and that industry and society have been dissociated. His alternative model views conflict as arising essentially from authority-subject relationships. Thus

> there are a large number of imperatively co-ordinated associations in any given society. Within every one of them we can distinguish the aggregates of those who dominate and those who are subjected.[19]

Men are seen to act

> in accordance not with their position in a class structure, but in accordance with their position in a pluralistic society wherein a range of authority-subject relationships determine action.[20]

To those competing perspectives of the basis of power must be added the elitist position—best summarised by C. Wright Mills' conceptualisation of the U.S. establishment as an

> internal power elite monolithic in structure, ruthlessly exploitive of men, driven only by quest for ever-renewed profit, arrayed against the downtrodden and poor who are denied access to the political levers by which change can be achieved.

The validity of these various approaches remains disputed. For example, has the growth of status groups and social mobility become such that Marx's conception of class has been considerably weakened? Critics disagree on both the amount and range of mobility and the criteria whereby to measure it. More easily falsified, as Bottomore (1965) notes, is Dahrendorf's view of a post-capitalist society within which industry and political conflict are institutionally isolated. Numerous studies have shown that

> the major political conflicts are closely and continuously associated with industrial conflicts, and express the divergent interests of the principal social classes.

It is possible, nevertheless, that there may be conflict groups in society besides social classes which at times assume great importance, but to resolve such issues is beyond the scope of this study. For present purposes it is sufficient to note that the types of groups and interests involved in conflict may in part depend upon the subject of dispute, and that in dealing with the pollution laws, an economic (class) division is likely to be more appropriate (since these laws govern the activities of certain powerful economic groups) than one concerned with authority-subject relations which falsely regards industrial conflict as divorced from political struggle.

Moreover, the concept of class is to be preferred to that of elite as a tool of analysis and as an explanation for the cohesion of a ruling group since, as Bottomore (1964) notes, an elite is *assumed* to be cohesive whereas a ruling class (here defined as the class which owns the major instruments of economic production in a society) is *shown* to be a cohesive social group because its members have economic interests in common and because it is permanently engaged in conflict with other classes in society.

Models of the Law-Making Process

Given a general model of society and of social struggle, we have yet to consider more closely the sort of groups or individuals who campaign for legislation and the factors which will bear on their degree of success. A useful starting point in such an examination is the concept of a social problem, because it is necessary to understand how something becomes a social problem in order to understand how legislation may subsequently arise.

Fuller and Myers assert that

> every social problem . . . consists of an objective condition and a subjective definition. The objective condition is a verifiable situation which can be checked as to its existence and magnitude by impartial and trained observers. The subjective definition is the awareness of certain individuals that the condition is a threat to certain cherished values. . . . Social problems are what people think they are,[21] and if conditions are not defined as social problems by the people involved in

23

them, they are not problems to these people although they may be problems to outsiders or scientists.

As Becker maintains, we must consider not only the objective condition but also the varying definitions of the problem by various groups that have an interest in it, because the definitions themselves play a role in giving a problem the form it has in society.

To Becker

> the first stage of a social problem comes when some person or group sees a set of objective conditions as problematic, posing a danger or containing the seeds of future difficulties. . . . After a problem comes to someone's attention, concern with it must be shared and widespread if it is to achieve the status of a social problem.

If legislation is to result, someone must have a strong enough interest in the enactment of the law to take the initiative and press for its passage. What he achieves will depend on his success in bringing the problem to the attention of others, in convincing them that the situation is dangerous enough to require public action, in defending his definitions against others, and on his access to the instruments of publicity and political power.

Becker uses the term 'moral entrepreneurs' to signify those individuals who unite together without direct interests in order to eliminate the social evils from society. These people must persuade others that the proposed law serves some recognised value of the society, and neutralize the objections of others whose interests will be adversely affected by the law. If he succeeds, the entrepreneur will have created a new fragment of the moral constitution of society.

Becker uses the 1937 Marijuana Tax Act to illustrate this. He shows that sustained and large scale moral enterprise provoked by the activities and ideology of the Federal Bureau of Narcotics, rather than the spontaneous recognition by Congress of self-evident evil, created the awareness of a major social problem and forced the subsequent legislation. He concludes that deviance is always the result of enterprise:

> before any act can be viewed as deviant, and before any class of people can be labelled as outsiders for committing the act, someone must have made the rule which defines the act as

24

deviant. Rules are not made automatically. Even though a practice may be harmful in an objective sense to the group in which it occurs, the harm needs to be discovered and pointed out. People must be made to feel that something ought to be done about it. Someone must call the public's attention to these matters, supply the push necessary to get things done, and direct such energies as are aroused in the proper direction to get a rule created.

An alternative view of the Marijuana Tax Act is that of D. J. Dickson, who argues that the Act was the result of a bureaucratic response to environmental pressure—that the Narcotics Bureau, faced with a non-supportive environment and a decreasing budgetary appropriation that threatened its survival, generated a crusade again Marijuana use which resulted in the passage of the Act and the alteration of a societal value. Such an organisational perspective may indeed be appropriate to some moral crusades involving bureaucracies with vested interests.

Comparing the emergence of the prohibition laws with those on drugs, both in terms of the forces bringing the laws into effect and in terms of the ability of the laws to withstand opposition, one finds a marked similarity. The prohibition laws largely represent

> the effective campaign of a small but highly vocal and well organised interest group convinced of the moral degeneration of the society which they believed stemmed from the availability of alcoholic beverages.[22]

There is little doubt that the efforts of this group of moral entrepreneurs did not in any sense represent the spirit of the time but were effective primarily because opposition to the movement was unorganised and apathetic. In this case the movement is seen, at least by Joseph Gusfield, not as an example of a class or economically powerful group imposing their interests on the law, but as an example of a status movement— "moral reform as a political and social issue—a moral issue divorced from direct economic interests in abstinence or indulgence . . . a quality of 'disinterested reform'."

Gusfield sees three types of reforming movement. A class structure is viewed as the system of relationships between the different classes in society, including their differential power and the extent of their organisation into politically relevant associations. Class politics is an effort to influence material gain, to rectify discontents by directly affecting the distribution of wealth, whereas 'expressive politics' is an arena in which "feelings, emotions and affect are displaced and expressed" rather than one in which an attempt is made to influence or control the distribution of valued objects. The third group in Gusfield's classification, and the one which he considers appropriate in analysing the temperance movement, he terms 'status politics'.

The crucial idea is that political action can, and often has, influenced the distribution of prestige. "Status politics is an effort to control the status of a group by acts which function to raise, lower or maintain the social status of the acting group *vis-à-vis* others in the society". Status movements can be distinguished from class and expressive movements by the nature of their goals and by the character of the group to whose values and welfare the movement is oriented. These movements appeal to the "not uncommon resentments of individuals or groups who desire to maintain or improve their social status", and status discontents are likely to appear when the prestige accorded to persons and groups by prestige givers is perceived as less than that which the person or group expects.[23]

Gusfield emphasises the importance of separating status and class movements, for

> how we perceive political struggles, as matters of class or of status, has a great bearing on the groups we perceive as parties to a political conflict. The thrust of status politics is precisely in identifying non-economic segments as crucial in certain social and political conflicts.

While recognising this distinction and the usefulness of the analysis of both Becker and Gusfield in terms of moral enterprise or symbolic crusade in explaining the moral "softening up" before legislation and of isolating important factors in the struggle to create new legislation, nevertheless one cannot explain the precipitation of legislation at large without mention of the vast numbers with personal, financial and material interests involved.

Becker's analysis particularly, is an example of what Lemert calls "the persuasive sociopsychological model which reduces the complexities of societal reaction to interpersonal interaction" and he characterises Becker's notion of the work of moral entrepreneurs as a type of *reductio ad personam* theory illustrations of which may be found . . . narrowly centering on issues like alcohol and drug use, gambling and sex, which are characterised by ambivalence, value conflict and the absence of victimisation. In decided contrast, the law of theft while at times affected by public opinion, scarcely can be said to have resulted from Moral Crusades.

A number of researches attest to the influence of vested interest and specialised associations in shaping criminal and regulatory legislation.

For Lemert, to understand the interplay of so many groups in the development of new categories of legal and moral control requires a model of group interaction rather than interpersonal interaction:

when a chain of interaction mediated by groups precedes decisions and actions, what is an end value for one person may be no more than an expendable means to another; hence predicting the societal reaction by taking the role of the other and intuiting what is in the mind of the civic reformer, legislator, etc., fails.

This leads him to suggest that a model of group interaction shifts from persons as such to interests, values or claims of others and to the order in which they are likely to be sacrificed in the light of group commitments, the availability of means and the costs of the means.

In particular, the role of technology must not be ignored as a limiting and imperative factor, and Lemert stresses that

the behaviour and verbal rationales of corporation executives can . . . only be understood . . . in the context of technological and cost imperatives that confront whole corporations

—a point to which we shall return later.

Limitations of Existing Models

Existing theorisation in criminal law, being largely concerned with enterprise on taken-for-granted criminality, seems to have focused on successful enterprise and law creation, without considering why laws are *not* created. An adequate theory should be concerned with explaining both moral enterprise, the lack of enterprise, and the lack of successful enterprise.

In studying the perceived problems of pollution, it is frequently the lack of legislation that demands attention. Existing literature, though of indirect bearing on this, may not adequately encompass the considerable debate *within* the powerful on the pollution issue, nor explain the unsuccessful attempts by individuals and groups to press legislation on the powerful, and may be of direct use only in explaining successful legislative campaigns. Nevertheless, by implication, the literature concerns unsuccessful entrepreneurial efforts. If the factors necessary to law creation are absent, then this in itself partly explains the lack of law.

With this background, subsequent chapters will seek to isolate the values, specific pressure groups and/or individuals involved in the struggle for pollution legislation. Their philosophies, their tactics, major strategies and success will be examined, and the evolution of environmental legislation will be related to the theoretical positions outlined in this chapter.

NOTES

1. Chambliss, W. J. and Seidman, B., 1971.
2. Taylor, I., Walton P. and Young, J., 1973.
3. Law under both divisions of labour is seen as representing the common conscience (though it will be broken more often under pathological social conditions), and it may not be a true and just consensus—as Taylor, Walton and Young have noted

   The collective conscience in a forced division of labour, far from being an idealization of social order, is a principle of 'justice' in which wealth is apportioned to men on a fundamentally inequitable base.

   Nevertheless, the law does represent some sort of consensus, and Durkheim is fundamentally bound to this assumption rather than to any concept of law as representing or perpetuating powerful interests.
4. Chambliss and Seidman, 1971.
5. Ibid.
6. Shkar, J., *Legalism.* Cambridge: Harvard Univ. Press, 1964.
7. Stone, J., *The Province and Function of Law.* Cambridge: Harvard Univ. Press, 1961.

8. Hall, J., 1960.
9. Chambliss, W. J., 1969.
10. Schur, E., 1968.
11. Friedmann, W., 1972.
12. Thus Wedgwood Benn asks "can you really run a democratic society if the instruments of mass communication fail to allow people to talk to other people about their problems fairly and openly and without distortion?" He alleges that "if the people were ever allowed to demonstrate that they were not apathetic and not violent but in fact highly intelligent and highly critical and would like certain things done, you would destroy at a single stroke the whole basis on which power in society now operates".
13. Taylor, Walton and Young, 1973.
14. "It is a corollary of the fact that every governmental system is itself the result of power relationships that the system of representation in the corridors of power will operate to the benefit of some interest groups and to the disadvantage of others" (Chambliss and Seidman, 1971) and legislation typically favours the wealthier, more politically active groups in the society.
15. Chambliss, W. J., 1969. For revised account of Chambliss's analysis of the law of vagrancy, see Chambliss, W. J. (1973) *Sociological Readings in the Conflict Perspective*. Addison-Wesley, pp. 430-444.
16. Carson, W. G., 1971.
17. Chambliss and Seidman, 1971. This view that the processes of the State, its costs, system of exclusions and success in legitimising the rulers, are all factors crucial in determining which particular interest groups will control the State itself, is supported by the Marxist concept of the State as consisting of the instruments of coercion.
18. Bottomore, T. D., 1964.
19. Dahrendorf, R., 1959.
20. Taylor, Walton and Young, 1973.
21. It is manifestly untrue to assert, as Fuller and Myers do, that there is no such thing as an objective social problem. Can man adapt to the destruction of his environment when the air becomes so poisoned he cannot breathe?
22. Chambliss, W. J., 1969.
23. In the case of the temperance movement, while not denying the importance of religious motives or moral fervour, these do not happen 'in vacuo' apart from the specific setting. Gusfield examines the social conditions which make the facts of other people's drinking especially galling to the abstainer and the need for reformist action acutely pressing to him. He concludes that these conditions are found in the development of threats to the socially dominant position of the temperance adherent by those whose style of life differs from his. As his own claim to social respect and honour are diminished, the sober abstaining citizen seeks public acts through which he may reaffirm the dominance and prestige of his style of life. Converting the sinner to virtue is one way, law is another. Even if the law is not enforced or enforceable, the symbolic import of its passage is important to the reformer.

Chapter Two: THE EMERGENCE OF ENVIRONMENTAL
CONSCIOUSNESS

It is important to understand how something becomes a social
problem in order to explain how legislation may subsequently
arise; an account of the evolution of pollution legislation must
include those precipitating factors which by themselves cannot
explain the passing of legislation, but without which the whole
ecological movement might not have begun.

Such an account cannot seek to explain current environmental
concern in terms only of a deteriorating environment, for
pollution has been with us for centuries, particularly in London.[1]
While there has been spasmodic legislation over environmental
problems over the past twenty-five years, it was not until the late
1960's that 'environment', 'pollution', and 'ecology' became issues
of national concern upon which Parliament took action. It is this
belated recognition of a problem by both public and Parliament
that must be explained.

The growing concern over pollution was partly a consequence
of the moral entrepreneurial activity of a number of individuals,
prominent amongst whom was Rachel Carson. Her book, *Silent
Spring,* succeeded in arousing widespread interest in pesticides,
both in America and Britain, by uncovering and pointing out
publicly for the first time the facts that link modern contaminants
to all parts of the environment. United States Government experts
have acknowledged that *Silent Spring* prompted the Federal
government to take action against water and air pollution—as
well as against persistent pesticides—several years before it would
otherwise have moved.

Rachel Carson epitomises the moral entrepreneur whose direct
interests are not involved. Because of her status as a writer, and
her scientific background, the pesticide controversy became a
subject of public debate and by the end of 1962 over forty Bills

30

had been introduced in the various state legislatures to regulate pesticide use.

In the years since *Silent Spring,* the environmental movement in America has been characterised by "prophets of doom, hot gospellers and ecological evangelists", chief amongst whom is Professor Paul Ehrlich whose book *The Population Bomb* sold over 1,250,000 copies.

Ehrlich and others have been aided by the mass media which in Western countries are placed in a competitive situation where they must constantly maintain and extent their circulation. To do this they must attract attention by taking up newsworthy material. A major component of newsworthiness is that which is emotive and which arouses public indignation, and the media have an institutionalised need to expose these kinds of social problems. In this context the media can try and arouse resentment at the activities of certain impersonal corporations whose success in ignoring or bending rules to their own ends can be represented either as damaging to a particular group of citizens (such as the people living or working near the R.T.Z. works at Avonmouth) or as damaging to society generally (the effects of D.D.T.).

The sensational way in which the media draws attention to, and creates problems, has been given impetus by the several nationwide private groups who have devoted considerable time and energy in recent years to convincing the public of the dangers of pollution. These have included voluntary groups of environmentalists,[2] such as the National Smoke Abatement Society and also the Conservation Society in Britain, which, since it was founded in 1966, has been committed to education and political pressure in the belief that unless the causes of the environmental crisis are known and understood, it will be impossible to mobilize the support to deal with them. Friends of the Earth, in both America and Britain, similarly devotes itself to substantial legislative activity, including lobbying and focusing attention on critical issues via the media.

The success of such groups and the effect of media exposure is demonstrated by the great increase in public concern in the past few years. One can look back at what has been described as a "two year immersion experience" by which the American public were made aware of the environment. T.V., radio, pop songs, advertising and the whole machinery of communications went into the ecology boom with such a will that the very clichés are now used to advertise consumer goods.

However, this does not explain why ecology became such a big issue when it did. If John Evelyn in 1661 was unable to convince people of the dangers of pollution, why should Carson or Ehrlich have been given widespread support and an enthusiastic reception in America? Why did pollution in the 1960's become such a social problem? A number of explanations, supplementary or alternative to that of moral enterprise, may provide the answer.

The massive growth in production which has characterised the American economy in the last two decades has contributed to intensification of the degree of actual pollution[3] and the problem today is very different from that of the past. By 1285 London had a smog problem arising from the burning of soft coal—but our present combustion of fossil fuels threatens to change the chemistry of the globe's atmosphere as a whole.

In recent years the eruption of environmental crises has also stirred the public not only to awareness of the dangers of environmental pollution, but also to demand that something be done about it. Thus the Torrie Canyon oil tanker disaster off the British coast, the effect of pesticides and chemicals in causing bird 'kills', the twenty deaths and illness of thousands attributed to a prolonged smog in Donata, Pennsylvania, and the London 'killer smog' of 1952, have all had a catalytic effect in various areas of pollution control. The passing of the 1956 Clean Air Act, as a result of the London smog, is direct evidence of the impact of these crises in provoking legislation.[4]

Furthermore, the ecology boom in America came about when the increase in the standard of living and rising social standards had permitted people the comparative luxury of being able to be concerned about pollution, and it could be that conservationist action by some sections of society represents a rejection as well as a surfeit of industrialism, and of affluence.

Moreover, just as the Marijuana Tax Act can be seen as the result not of moral enterprise but of a bureaucratic response by the Federal Narcotics Bureau to boost its own waning power and prestige, so it is possible that the growth of modern technology may have brought with it not only an increase in the amount of pollution but also a special group of experts in whose interests

32

it is to define pollution as a serious and actionable social problem. It could be, for example, that unaffiliated, largely academic, natural scientists, by detailed empirical examinations, are able to show significant ecological changes caused by pollution, and that generalisations from the natural to the social world have led to pollution becoming labelled as a social problem. When this occurs, more funds and prestige move into the hands of those experts who have been defined (perhaps by themselves) as qualified to deal with the situation. The process may be seen as one made possible by a complex bureaucratic society which is motivated by desire for status and power rather than by direct material interest.

Certainly awareness of pollution has been heightened in recent years by our capacity to measure its harmful effects in a way not possible in the past. Statistics linking pollution and health, comparisons of mortality rates and our knowledge about respiratory disease, have all been markedly increased by the work of the Medical Research Council, the T.U.C., the medical profession working in industry and general medical research. But to what extent present concern has been 'manufactured' by the experts in their own interests remains a matter of speculation, and in the absence of substantial evidence it would be most unjust to attribute machiavellian motives to those whose efforts have enabled a sharper appreciation of the effects of pollution on health.

Material interest groups have been conspicuously absent from this analysis of the generation of environmental concern. While these may well affect the outcome of environmental pressure, it is not suggested that the initial generation of concern was caused by such groups. Indeed, since these largely governmental and industrial groups are concerned with maintaining their own goals within the legal, political and economic status quo, it is only when their interests are directly threatened by pollution control measures that one might expect them to act. Until such time, they have no reason to be involved in the evolution of this new social problem.[5]

Thus, to explain the emergence of environmental consciousness and the demand for legislation we must look elsewhere. The evidence put forward in this chapter suggests that the initial concern for the environment was produced partly by a number

33

of inter-related facets of modern industrial society—a worsening environment, increasing affluence (and reaction to this), sharper appreciation of the effects of pollution on health through the use of modern research methods—and partly by the response to these factors by social reformers (either individual moral entrepreneurs or groups) whose efforts have been aided by the tendencies of the mass communications media to sensationalise newsworthy material and disseminate it widely throughout society.

NOTES

1. Thus in 1661, John Evelyn attacked

   the sordid and accursed avarice of some few particular persons [which makes] the inhabitants breath nothing but an impure and thick mist, accompanied by a fuliginous and filthy vapour . . . corrupting the lungs and disordering the entire habit of their bodies.

   However, fogs continued and no action was taken after the increasing mortality which accompanied the major London fogs of 1873, 1880, 1882, 1891, 1892, 1935 and 1948. A committee investigating London's serious air pollution problem in the early 1920's wrote "We have never ceased to bear in mind that the interests of trade must be fully considered, and that the introduction of legislation which might prejudicially affect important industries is quite out of the question". Not until the disaster of the 1952 Great Smog of London was action taken.
2. These groups generally consist of individuals united only in their concern about the environment. They seem to be genuinely disinterested social reformers whose success would bring them no material gain—though the Smoke Abatement Society did include, and was partly financed by, manufacturers of smokeless fuels.
3. As technology advances, more toxic materials are used, often in dangerous processes. As the Club of Rome recently illustrated, the rate of increase in pollution is greater than linear and can in one sense be regarded almost as exponential.
4. This will be considered later.
5. The only economic interest groups who might be involved at an earlier stage (except for the producers of smokeless fuel) are those concerned with making pollution control equipment. But these products were not marketed until it was appreciated that there would be a demand, and these interests are more likely to be a result of, rather than a cause of, environmental concern.

Chapter Three: THE STRUGGLE FOR LEGISLATION:
THE GROUPS INVOLVED

To explain the growth of environmental concern and the demand
for legislation is not necessarily to explain the emergence of
legislation. Only some legislative campaigns are successful, others
fail. Various explanations account for such a campaign, and for
its outcome. First, it may be the result of consensus—of a general
value change leading to a consensual demand for certain legislation. If so, then the outcome will depend upon whether the
political system enables consensual views to be implemented in
legislation. Second, if such an analysis proves false, if no consensus exists, then a campaign for legislation will involve conflicting groups, some demanding change and others resisting it. In
this case also, the outcome will depend upon the political system,
upon the relationships of power within the social structure, upon
those who are able to implement their views through legislation.

In the case of pollution, the former position is untenable.
Although awareness of pollution has increased in recent years,
this has not resulted in any general value change in society, and
a number of competing definitions of, and solutions to, the
pollution problem are presently maintained by various groups.

Thus at one extreme are those who regard pollution as a minor
problem and who deny that the environment is being threatened,
while at the other, it is suggested that overpopulation, exploitation of natural resources and pollution will cause eco-catastrophe
if present policies are not drastically amended. From this perspective it is claimed that the capitalist market economy has not,
and cannot, deal with the environmental problems we are facing.
Thus *The Ecologist* magazine's "Blueprint for Survival" alleges
that

> The principal defect of the industrial way of life with its ethos
> of expansion is that it is not sustainable . . . if current trends

35

are allowed to persist, the breakdown of society and the irreversible disruption of the life support systems of this planet . . . are inevitable.[1]

Somewhere between the extremes is the 'moderate' position which argues that we must balance the benefits of industry against its undesirable consequences, and that given sufficient funds, the problem can be cleared up without changing the prevailing aims and policies of our society. The Royal Commission on Environmental Pollution sees the problem as "how to strike a balance between the benefits gained from economic and technical achievements and what is being lost in terms of deterioration of the environment".[2]

Thus it is apparent that we cannot establish a working consensus on the practice of pollution control,[3] and thereby explain the demand for, and possible emergence of, legislation.[4] Instead, we must examine the various competing interests and pressure groups involved in the debate over pollution control and categorise them in terms of their motives, aims, and relative power. Later, this will enable us to consider whose interests are implemented in law, to help explain the relationship between social structure and criminal law, to see at what point the balance of power is struck and whether this is the result of pluralism (the politics of consensus) or conflict.

Interest Groups and the Law

Those groups and individuals who have demanded stricter pollution control can broadly be classified into four types—social reformers, expressive movements, status movements and 'middle range' power groups. In the first category are those groups and individual moral entrepreneurs who were described in the previous chapter. Their success in provoking environmental concern and in creating a moral climate will not necessarily generate legislation, although the larger American conservation groups—such as the National Wildlife Federation (with an estimated 2,500,000 supporters)—may have some impact on occasion.

In the second group are those new 'deviant' types involved in what Gouldner calls Modern Psychedelic Romanticism. These

36

include the beats, hippies, acid heads, dropouts, and the 'New Left', who have emerged during the post-war period of affluence. Because the state has failed to incorporate the psychedelic romantics tightly into the economic structure, they exist in a limbo of their own choosing. Rejecting the rewards offered by society as insufficient to warrant conformity, they have evolved social theories of an articulate and ideological nature, rejective of the system, which uphold subterranean values as authentic guides to action.

These theories attempt to solve the problem of the dominance of the ethos of productivity by rejecting the central values to which all variants of industrial society are committed. As such, they have embraced pollution as an anti-materialistic issue implicating capitalist industrial society. In accordance with their cultural ethos, their opposition has been in non-utilitarian terms, "In short, many, particularly among the young, are now orienting themselves increasingly to expressive rather than instrumental politics".[5] As such, their impact on the resolution of conflict is predictably small,[6] particularly in Britain, where the youth culture, retaining ties with the economic structure, lacks the strength it has in America.

Others involved in pollution control could include status groups of unaffiliated specialists who see the ecological changes caused by pollution as harmful, and view themselves as qualified to deal with 'the problem'. Only limited evidence exists, none of which is strong enough to establish the motives of the experts concerned. What can be said is that, for whatever reasons, scientists have indeed become more involved—particularly the American Academy for the Advancement of Science (which has established an Air Conservation Commission), health groups, and those concerned about the social implications of technological advance.

More materially involved in the drive for control at a national level are the U.S. Conference of Mayors, the National League of Cities, and the National Association of Counties. Davies' explanation for this is that,

the cities and suburbs have been faced with the necessity of undertaking major expenditure for the laying of sewer lines and the construction of water treatment plants. Thus their major stake in Federal legislation has been to get Washington to commit more Federal funds for their purposes. . . . Their

37

interest coincides with that of the conservation groups, who tend to see Federal resources as the only hope for stimulating sufficient investment to curb water pollution significantly. The municipal and county groups have also looked upon Federal action as the primary means of ensuring that the pollution control efforts of one municipality will not be undercut by the lack of such efforts in a neighbouring community.

Both these groups and the articulate middle class pressure groups in Britain [7] may best be seen as examples of what Wright Mills calls the middle levels of society. These, on the fringes of the power elite in America, include "the rank and file of Congress, the pressure groups that are not vested in the power elite itself, as well as the multiplicity of regional, state and local interests". These latter are concerned mainly with their particular cut, with their particular area of vested interest, and are often of no decisive political importance.

Significantly absent from environmental politics is any class movement. Although the burden of pollution problems falls, and has always fallen, on the working classes, they have taken little interest in environmental problems, not only because the cost of measures to overcome pollution fall disproportionately on them, but also because they have traditionally used the trade unions to redress grievances, and the trade unions are occupied with more basic matters at present. A further obstacle to any demands for a cleaner environment is the loss of jobs that may follow the discontinuation of the polluting product.

Some have suggested that conservationist concerns manifest a set of middle and upper class value-judgements, that environmentalists are those who have already reaped the benefits of industrial growth and can afford to campaign for their own protection. Nevertheless, few environmentalists have a vested class interest in the environment that is not shared by the less wealthy, and the domination of conservation bodies by the middle class can be attributed rather to their greater awareness of the channels of communication, which they, being articulate, are more able to manipulate. The campaign for pollution control thus defies class classification; it is not the approach of a dominant social class to those less favourably situated in the economic and social structure (a movement from above), yet neither can one regard it as a movement from below.

More easily classified within a class structure are those groups to be found in opposition to pollution control, the most important of which are capitalists with strong economic interests in maintaining the status quo. These are involved because in a capitalist market economy, the organisation of economic activity has historically been based on numerous fragmented units, each seeking to operate as profitably as possible, while paying only the costs which it is impossible to avoid. Thus the dilemma of the polluting industry is that controlling pollution is expensive, but adds nothing to the value of the goods produced, and is bad business for any firm whose main concern is to maintain a level of profit in a competitive situation.[8] Since the enforcement of more extensive legislation would attack the very root of capitalism (i.e. profit and the self-expansion of all capital, large or small, by the 'fair purchase and consumption of labour power'), the capitalist class must oppose strict pollution control measures in as much as they threaten this objective.

The extent to which industry has felt it necessary to oppose pollution control, and their motives for so doing, will be more closely examined later, but it may be observed here that in resisting pressure for pollution control, the interests of government and industry have coincided,[9] and one must consider "how far the various formally separate groups among which power is distributed represent in fact, not distinct and competing interests, but broadly similar interests in different institutional dress".[10]

Certain government agencies involved in status politics also have a vested interest in opposing pollution control. Status discontents are most likely to appear when the prestige accorded to persons or groups by prestige givers is perceived as less than that which the person or group deserves. It may frequently be a bureaucratic response of the kind that Dickson suggests would account for the passing of the Marijuana Tax Act. In the pollution campaign, the clearest example of an agency engaged in status politics is the U.S. Department of Agriculture (U.S.D.A.), whose irresponsible attitude towards pesticides has been severely criticised.

Why U.S.D.A. went overboard on new pesticides can be understood within an organisational perspective. The department found its power and responsibilities diminishing in comparison with several other departments. Graham notes how the twentieth century has reached the farm, and the successful farmer-business-man, with his vast acreage, college degree and modern machinery, was less dependent on U.S.D.A. than the poorly educated struggling farmer with his scanty crop a decade or two earlier. U.S.D.A. then

> reacted in the tradition of all bureaucracies which feel their position threatened by shrinking responsibilities. The depart-ment's impulse to fabricate programs which gave it the illusion of 'business' has been especially apparent . . . in the business of promoting pesticides, springing to arms at the first whisper of a pest.[11]

However, once a government has taken action on pollution the fact that something has been done may create a demand for further action because the public learn that something can be done. Once an official agency has been established to control pollution, it becomes a focal point for bringing the issue to the attention of the general public and government officials. Members of the agency have a vested interest in drawing attention to the problem. The concern with pollution will become institutionalised and the pressure to take action will be constant, because private interest groups may take up the call to action and public concern will in turn strengthen the hand of the governmental agency.[12]

NOTES

1. *The Ecologist* Vol. 2 No. 1 January, 1972.
2. Royal Commission on Environmental Pollution. First Report, 1971.
3. Although if all other things were equal, almost everyone would choose to eliminate pollution, the investments or sacrifices which would be necessary would prevent the powerful in society from pursuing many other goals and values they (or some of them) have set themselves. Thus, as Davies notes, any government body faced with the job of establishing and enforcing standards, must weigh the costs of control-ling pollution against the costs of other goals—housing, education, economic growth, etc.
4. Nor can we give an objective assessment of the adequacy of the present pollution control legislation because the word pollution is value-laden, because the control of pollution is a political problem,

and because the very definition of the word pollution hinges on individual conception. How one views pollution, and what level of it one should tolerate, depends upon what one wants to do with the environment, and in the event of conflict between groups and interpretations, then rightness becomes a practical matter of power and political persuasion.

5. Gouldner, A., 1971.
6. This need not always be so. Expressivity need not necessarily be non-instrumental in political impact—arguably the Hippies had a cultural impact on the culture of a generation, which in turn could face structural change.
7. The motives of these groups are mixed, but they are overtly economic when pressure groups are formed on such limited issues as airport and motorway sitings (which threaten to cause financial loss to local property owners).
8. At present, pollution's main economic characteristic is that its costs are not usually borne by the polluters, so that production is often pushed beyond the socially optimum point. There is inadequate incentive to allocate sufficient resources to reducing pollution and certain producers and consumers benefit at the expense of the victims of pollution.
9. The significance of pollution control as a vote-catching issue, particularly in America, might lead one to expect a strong governmental attack on pollution were it not that to do so would be contrary to a number of other objectives of government.

   Rattray Taylor (1970) notes that governments are anxious to balance their budgets, which they find easier in conditions of industrial expansion. They are also anxious to balance their overseas trade and in both cases, if they have to choose between amenity and industry, always favour the latter. Even if governments are compelled to act on pollution, their solution is likely to be a mild interference with the present system rather than a far more radical reversal of our allegedly destructive technology and acquistic growth technology.

   In Britain "both major political parties appear to be mesmerised by two dominating notions: that economic expansion is essential for survival and is the best possible index of progress and well being; and that unless solutions can be devised that do not threaten this notion, then the problems should not be regarded as existing. Unfortunately, government has an increasingly powerful incentive for continued expansion in the tendency of economic growth to create the need for more economic growth". *The Ecologist* Vol. 2 No. 1, 1972.

10. Westergaard, J., 1966.
11. Graham, F. Jnr., 1970.
12. See Davies, J. C., 1970.

Chapter Four: INDUSTRY'S RESPONSE TO THE ENVIRON-MENT, PAST AND PRESENT

Subsequent examination of specific legislation will suggest that the role of industry is of great importance in influencing the outcome of legislative campaigns. This being so, it is important to understand and explain industry's current position on the pollution issue.

In 1956, when the Clean Air Act was passed, industry was predominantly hostile to effective anti-pollution legislation in as much as this represented increased costs without any direct dividend, and the 'social conscience' of the majority was such that they were as prepared as ever to pass on some of the costs of production to the general public, rather than accept responsibility themselves.[1]

For most of industry, any re-allocation of resources to take account of pollution has been of more recent origin, and it is only in the last decade that many large industries have come to take the pollution problem seriously, and have become willing to take measures to reduce it without coercion or outside pressure. Thus the Chief Inspector of Alkali has remarked how often the Inspectorate found themselves preaching to the converted when meeting representatives of large industrial organisations, trade associations and nationalised industries—but smaller firms have presented a bigger problem.

For those who believe that in a competitive market economy a firm cannot devote a material part of its resources to unprofitable activities and survive, and that to believe in a firm's 'social conscience' in such a situation is naïve, then the apparently voluntary efforts and expenditure of some of the larger industrialists[2] are difficult to explain, as is the seemingly more responsible attitude that has been adopted by many large industrial concerns in recent years. Why, for example, did the requirements of the 1968 Clean Air Act meet so little opposition[3] from industry compared to those of its predecessor in 1956?

Two possible answers to be considered subsequently are that the legislation is still inadequate and that it is so inadequately enforced as to be ineffective in controlling industry. But whatever the weight of these factors, they do not explain the voluntary spending of a number of industries on pollution control.[4]

This cannot be explained without some theory of social structure—specifically of the state of capitalism in modern Western society, and of Burnham's theory of managerial capitalism. This asserts that whereas in the past, society has been organised through a certain set of major (capitalist) social and political institutions, and that within this social structure the capitalist class or bourgeoisie was the dominant ruling class, now, that ruling class is divided between owners and managers. In this structure of institutions and beliefs a transition is alleged whereby a different set of major economic, social and political institutions exhibiting different social beliefs and ideologies has emerged, and the managers have become the dominant or ruling class.

> There is a combined shift: through changes in the technique of production, the functions of management become more distinctive, more complex, more specialised, and more crucial to the whole process of production, thus serving to set off those who perform these functions as a separate group or class in society.

The growth of large scale public corporations along with the technological development of modern society has virtually wiped away, in important sections of the economy, the typical capitalist who is his own manager, and control has passed into the hands of salaried managers.

Thus ownership no longer affords a decisive element of economic power and in the last few decades the separation of ownership and control, at least in large scale enterprises, has become one of the most important features of the internal organisation of capitalist enterprise, although the process is far from complete.[5] This managerial element is largely immune from the control and even from the effective pressure of individual shareholders,[6] but financial capitalists owning a substantial block of shares may, like executives, have substantial legal interests in ownership of the company, and more power. Their aims are unlikely to coincide with those of the managers and the separation of ownership and control is a source of frequent conflict because, as Burnham notes,

> the position, role and function of the managers are in no way dependent upon the maintenance of capitalist property and economic relations but are dependent upon the technical nature of the process of modern production.

The manager's concern will be in some regulation of the quality, kinds, numbers and distribution of products apart from the technical abilities of the instruments of production to turn products out. This regulation "would not have to be achieved, however, in terms of capitalist profits for the company. It would be done in subordination to some political, social or psychological aim".

According to some exponents of the theory of managerial capitalism, managerial aims tend to be less 'selfish', more socially 'responsible' and more concerned with the public interest than old-style owner-capitalism. For example,

> now perhaps most typical amongst very large firms, is the company which pursues rapid growth and high profits—but subject to its 'sense of social responsibility' and desire for good public and labour relations.[7]

Such a view has not gone undisputed.[8] Arbitrary speculation about the personal motives of managers is of little value but it is important to recognise the pressures upon managers in corporate situations. Here, as Lemert has shown, the concept of costs is important.

> Costs are important variables in analysis because changes in the costs of means can modify the order of choice, even though the 'ideal' values order of the individual remains constant.

Unless the individual has the means for satisfying his values at costs corresponding to his wishes, then something will have to be sacrificed.

Thus although a manager may believe in pollution control, he may not implement his beliefs (even if he has the power). Group pressures in favour of high profits, particularly in a declining economy, may be strong, and he may come to see others, whose value hierarchies differ from his own (perhaps owners committed

44

to high profits), as means whereby to achieve his own ends. If these ends include career aspirations then the manager must acknowledge the hierarchy. He becomes, in effect, 'captured' by the claims of the association to which he has given allegiance and he is further captured (according to Miliband) by an inherent demand in the system of which the manager is both master and servant. This is that managers shall make the highest possible profits for their own enterprises: "this is what ultimately their power is for, and to it must be subordinated all other considerations, including the public welfare".

In addition to these pressures, it is significant that top managers in industry, the controllers and top executives in whose hands the major strategic policy decisions lie, are, at least in America, owners of large shareholdings themselves. "It is hard to believe that, as wealthy shareholders, they voluntarily allow their policies to be dictated to by considerations conflicting with those of long term profit maximisation" [9] and "those few directors and managers who have no important shareholding are still likely to be tied to the owners by their aspirations and values, by a respect for the institution of property and by a common social background".[10]

Moreover it must not be forgotten that the ultimate goal of capitalism as a system is the accumulation of capital and the making of profit, and that, as Blackburn notes, the actual mechanisms of the capitalist economy are not subordinated to human control. "If managerial decisions must be vindicated in market terms, any failure within the market will frustrate almost any kind of personal ambition".

However, while one must accept that managers cannot be totally unconcerned with profit, inasmuch as a corporation cannot run at a loss and survive, this is the limit of the manager's short term concern with profit. Otherwise the manager, by his position, appointment and technical function, is relatively free from the immediate pressures and interest in high profitability and is able to think in the long term. In such cases he may consider it in the company's own interests to instigate pollution control measures.

In making this decision it must not be assumed that he will automatically meet opposition and resistance from owners[11] and shareholders; they may reach the same conclusion (or be persuaded to). Nowadays the latter often hold shares in a number of firms, are not tied to the immediate fortunes of any one, and may themselves be more concerned with sustained, consistent long term profits than with a quick 'killing'. The managers (at least in the larger corporations with larger research facilities and the chance to make contingency plans for the future), because of their technical knowledge of the firm's behaviour and its possible impact on the environment, are more likely to be concerned with its long term implications. Some are also more likely to be convinced that the company's behaviour is harmful because, being salaried and often in Britain without owning shares, they do not have the same interest in maintaining the company's present mode of behaviour as have the owners and shareholders.

Thus, where a firm can afford to implement pollution controls and still make a sufficient profit to maintain expansion, research etc, we may expect it to do so if it perceives it to be in its own long term interests. Why voluntary spending on control has only been evident occasionally in the last twenty years, somewhat more frequently in the last decade, may be explained partly because the managers previously did not have so much power, but more likely because managers and owners previously failed to see the significance and possible consequences of environmental pollution.

> It has become apparent with dramatic suddenness that, at the present more or less uncontrolled rate of industrial and urban development, the major rivers and lakes of the country will become incapable of supporting marine life and unsuitable for humans.[12]

Car exhaust emissions, factory chimneys and industrial processes are poisoning the air, mercury and other industrial by-products are making fish unfit for human consumption, and the increase in production of carbon monoxide is affecting photosynthesis and the temperature of the earth.

When the potential power of the growing environmental lobby is realised, when firms face a possible total ban on their activities as the result of a future ecological disaster and public outcry, then those capable of being concerned with more than the immediate return to the company, those concerned with the company's future, may voluntarily impose pollution controls.

46

'Those capable' are those who can undertake pollution control within the confines of the profit margin, which can be reduced but not eliminated.[13] Since too, technological factors and costs are likely to be a limiting and influential aspect of pollution control policies, it is important to note that large, capital-intensive corporations in particular have sufficient financial resources to be able to allocate money for pollution abatement, and their larger research facilities enable them to recognise wider implications of their activities and to tackle them[14] (which often require sophisticated and expensive machinery). These companies by reason of their advanced technical and administrative problems, are more frequently and effectively controlled by managers.

However, the way in which a firm is likely to react to pollution depends on other factors as well as its economic position. In the absence of effective enforcement of pollution control legislation, many large wealthy firms (particularly competing transnational companies[15]) are still very reluctant to spend voluntarily on pollution control. Private companies, having no need to worry about stock market reaction to profits, can invest some profit into longer term goals of a social nature, like pollution control. Public companies, experiencing a greater pressure for short term profit,[16] require a stronger will to look beyond this to long term aims which do not necessarily have a financial pay-off.

Also of significance to a company's activities is the attitude of its competitors to the issue of pollution control. In one sense, a manufacturer does not mind how high his costs are, providing his competitors have the same costs. Thus one industrialist will be deterred from spending money to control pollution if others do not, and except in near monopoly situations, legislation may be the only way to stop the degeneration whereby the 'worst' drag the 'best' down to their level.

Other factors which may affect the way a company operates, and which tend to influence general patterns of behaviour, include its political influence, fiscal measures, public bodies such as the British Institute of Management and the Confederation of British Industries, trades unionism, information and control systems,[17] and the sensitivity of the firm to public opinion. With this latter, one must distinguish between those in whose interests it is to control pollution, and those in whose interests it is to appear to do so.

Those whose activities may in the future be directly banned (such as Monsanto) are more likely to control pollution than those whose pollution will have only indirect effects on their enterprise.[18] In Northern Italy at the moment, businesses are spending a lot of money on water pollution control equipment, and advertising the fact to show just how socially responsible they are. In fact they are running out of usable water and their choice is either to spend the money or close down.[19] The pollution situation is not generally that serious in Britain, but in a worsening environment the implications for British firms should not make it too difficult to see that control is often in their own long term interest. Producers of D.D.T. can no longer profit from it, because its irresponsible use has caused total ban. Perhaps the lesson is being learned, although empirical validation is necessary to substantiate this.

Others—frequently large firms selling under their own name—are more conscious of public relations and the need to appear to be doing something about pollution. Such firms have often taken the lead in publicising the need for pollution control, as have those who manufacture their own pollution control machinery and who need to maintain a 'clean' public image.

Many such firms may be engaged not in any genuine pollution control but only in image management. *The Ecologist* has suggested that a recent advertising ploy is to photograph the clean water upstream from a factory, giving the impression of pollution-free industry, while the water downstream continues to be systematically polluted. Certainly much advertising, particularly in America, stresses health, beauty, youth, the 'pure' things of life,[20] without hinting at the harmful side effects or polluting activities of the corporations concerned.

Perhaps the best example of a firm engaged in image management—of a firm advertising a 'clean image' in order to hide its own systematic polluting—is the Rio Tinto Zinc Corporation, a world wide mining and natural resources company. Recent examinations[21] of R.T.Z. suggest that it conceals its true motivations, with their social and environmental cost, behind a veneer of plausibility. Although establishing a company's true motivations is extremely difficult, these examinations have served to reveal the true nature of the group through its actions. Thus its chairman's report in 1971 dwells on its environmental triumphs in Canada and the U.S.A., where legislation on pollution control is both strict and enforced. The report makes no mention of an ecological disaster at Bourgainville, and there is a considerable gap between what the company says and what it does. Sir Val Duncan's remark at Avonmouth "R.T.Z. policy has always been, and will always be, the necessity to avoid endangering the health of any of our employees" bears little resemblance to the truth of numerous reports exposing health hazards over a considerable period, and a senior executive's admission that the building of the Avonmouth works was skimped.[22]

These and other incidents, have led a recent commentator to suggest that "what is clear is that R.T.Z.'s publicity machine will trim its sails to the prevailing winds but the company will not be diverted from its profit making course".[23]

Economic Competition and Control

Firms willing to solve or reduce the pollution problem voluntarily will be unfairly penalised if their smaller brethren continue to be allowed to pass on to the public part of their production cost. On the other hand, the small firm operating on a narrow profit margin might be forced out of business if it had to adopt anti-pollution measures. If the larger firms perceive it to be in their interests not only to control pollution, but also to force their smaller competitors out of business, then legislation might be seen as a useful weapon with which to achieve these ends.

Some commentators expect this to be the case. W. G. Carson considers

it would not be in the least surprising if . . . investigations of the current pressure for legislation which may well impose criminal sanctions on pollution, were to reveal that the competitive interests of some large scale industrial combines were every bit as significant in this movement as any universal awakening to the imminence of man's self-destruction.

Although the Factory Acts have been analysed this way, there is no indication of whether this is occurring in relation to pollution. At present the nature of enforcement activity is that the understaffed Alkali Inspectorate cannot hope to deal with all

49

firms and therefore concentrates on the larger and potentially more important polluters. Furthermore, they prosecute not when a firm cannot afford pollution control equipment, but when it can but refuses. Thus, to cut out smaller competitors by means of legislation, larger firms would have to lobby for stricter laws with a different, more severe and more efficient policy of enforcement. If they succeeded, this might indeed serve to put smaller competitors out of business. However, this is a drastic step which would involve the State interfering in industry's affairs and sphere of activities (an unattractive proposition to many industrialists). It only becomes viable when competitive margins are narrowing, when smaller firms offer direct economic competition. In other circumstances, when competitive margins are widening, when bigger firms are succeeding anyway, then action (if any) is more likely to be effective in the form of a take-over.

In America, voluntary restraint and spending on pollution control by industry is not always so evident. The automobile industry, for example, has totally resisted attempts to legislate against noxious exhaust fumes on the grounds of cost and the absence of any control technology capable of dealing with the problem. This is despite the possibility that some American cities will otherwise become so seriously polluted as to result in the banning of cars from them, which may mean a drop in sales.

It can only be said, following Caldwell, that it is easier to ascertain whose purposes are being served than whose interests:

> history is filled with examples of dominant groups who injured themselves in pursuit of purposes that not only were not in their best interests but contributed to their downfall; and because politically dominant groups are able to make their purposes public purposes, we find governments in the U.S. and elsewhere in vigorous pursuit of policies that could be said to be in the public interest only by legal definition.

To explain why in Britain big industry sometimes seems more willing to deal with pollution, one is perhaps forced back to an explanation in terms of values. In Britain, the physical constraints of living on an island of limited space and resources, have created an awareness of the dangers of pollution which has been conspicuously lacking in America where

> the pioneer experience, the frontier tradition, individualism, the illusion of endless natural wealth and a strongly materialistic

set of values has culminated in a social attitude that has long inhibited public efforts to protect or manage the natural environment.[24]

The failure of the American labour movement to develop a permanent and coherent political arm has also resulted in the power of private property being subjected to far fewer restrictions than generally obtain elsewhere.

Any measures proposed or adopted are conditioned by the initial assumption that entrenched rights of private ownership and private profit are sacrosanct to an extent inconceivable even to conservative parties in most other advanced capitalist societies.[25]

It is also much more common for managers in America to have stock in their companies. Stock options are often used as an incentive in a man's salary to encourage a real attack on profits and growth and this could well be a factor in the less responsible attitude to pollution of which there is some evidence.[26]

NOTES

1. However, even in this period there were exceptions, particularly the nationalised industries, whose involvement in pollution control was evident even earlier. Thus the 1957 Electricity Act put a statutory obligation on the Electricity Board to take account of environmental protection, although the industry was heavily involved in the area before the Bill, and has since been the biggest single spender on air pollution control, with a bill of £120 million over the last decade.

   Some parts of British industry have been concerned with the preservation of the environment on a significant scale for at least twenty years, and large sums have been spent to this end. The Steel Industry has spent £29 million on the prevention of smoke, grit, fumes and sulphurous gases since the introduction of the 1956 Clean Air Act, and the industry's switch to the use of high-purity oxygen as a refining agent in steelmaking has necessitated the expenditure of some £22 million extra on purification plant intended to eliminate fumes and excess carbon monoxide. *Financial Times,* 21.10.71.

2. Nevertheless there is evidence that such efforts are being made—the activities of Monsanto Chemicals Ltd., may be an example. In 1971, as sole North American and British manufacturers of the toxic and

highly persistent group of industrial organo-chlorine chemicals called P.C.B.'s, Monsanto voluntarily and drastically curtailed its sales of these substances so as to minimise the risk of further environmental contamination. Certainly such drastic action by a corporation is rare, but it serves as a good illustration of the kinds of specific factors which may make a corporation 'voluntarily' indulge in pollution control.

Jon Tinker (*New Scientist and Science Journal* 1.4.71) views Monsanto's move as "a last desperate throw to retain at least part of a lucrative market which might otherwise be entirely lost". Indeed, the company makes no effort to deny that it believes the partial P.C.B. ban to be in its own long term interests, and admits to being in the business to profit and prosper. So the objective fact that P.C.B.'s are harmful is not the sole reason for their action. Four additional reasons have been advanced and summarised by Tinker.

Monsanto feel certain that pressure to restrict P.C.B.'s will come sooner or later, and prefer to be masters of their own fate.

> This is probably a stronger argument in the U.S. than in Britain. Although both countries would need to legislate to ban P.C.B.'s, such legislation could not be enacted very quickly. The U.S. political system embodies such inordinate respect for authority that the President could probably bludgeon Monsanto into a 'voluntary' ban.

Monsanto scientists are under no illusions as to the strength of the environmental lobby: they were manufacturers of cyclamates, which were banned as a result of pressure.

Monsanto also feels that P.C.B.'s in the electrical industry are controllable and need cause no environmental contamination. Once governments start arm twisting, these applications might well disappear, together with those which do cause pollution. Monsanto is also anxious to market the anti-pollution technology which it has been forced to develop and a clean environmental sheet would help. Its monopoly position in America and Britain further means that it can act altruistically without too much risk of its competitors taking its place.

3. Mr. Robert Maxwell, introducing the Bill, said that "the coal merchants, the Confederation of British Industry, the National Coal Board and many other interested organisations have given the Bill a ready understanding . . . it is thought unlikely that there will be opposition to the principles of the Bill from these or other influential quarters". *Hansard*, p. 1802, 2nd February, 1968.

4. A recent example is Unilever, who have announced their intention to spend about £50 million on plant to deal with pollution in the next ten years. *The Guardian*, 10.5.73.

5. It has been noted of the U.S. (R. Sheehan, 'Proprietors in the World of Big Business' in *Fortune*, 15th June, 1967) that in approximately 150 companies on the current list of the 500 largest industrial corporations, controlling ownership rests in the hands of an individual or of the members of a single family. Nevertheless at the head of the largest, most dynamic and powerful concerns of the system are now to be found, and will increasingly be found, managers and executives who owe their position not to ownership but to appointment and co-option.

6. Except for the minor element of control involved in the preferential sharing of the profits.

7. Crosland, C. A. R., *The Conservative Enemy.*
8. cf. Miliband, R., 1969. Pearce, F., 'Crime, Corporations and the American Social Order', in Taylor and Taylor eds. *Politics and Deviance.* Penguin, 1973.
9. Westergaard, J., 1966.
10. Mills, C. W., 1956.
11. In Britain the passage of the various regulations concerning working conditions in factories can be seen in terms of large scale (owner controlled) industry pragmatically supporting such regulation because it was bad economic sense to train and discipline workers who soon after they reached their peak of efficiency might be rendered unproductive through industrial accident. On this issue (as with pollution) there was a conflict between the large and the small proprietors who feared they would be forced out of business.
12. Friedmann, W., 1972.
13. Except in the case of the nationalised industries whose spending on pollution emphasises their ability to take account of considerations other than profit alone.
14. Industries will only undertake control sufficient to ensure their continued existence in business. There is no evidence that they are concerned to create a clean environment as a matter of 'social conscience', though it would be facile to assume that industrialists were always motivated by long or short term profit.
15. Such corporations, lacking strong ties to particular States, cannot be pressurised by the threat of adverse legislation unless this is liable to have international implications.
16. The profitability of a company quoted on the stock exchange will affect its borrowing power and is thus of great significance to its policies.
17. In most large companies management control and information systems exist which, starting from the annual budget, measure (usually on a monthly basis) the way in which the business is progressing. The language for these systems is usually money and this is not a language that readily expresses the social implications of the company's activities such as pollution. Thus collective management will often be more concerned with profit than any other objectives of the company.
18. In some cases those who spend money reducing pollution may not be the people who gain from resulting improvement of the environment, e.g., sewage works benefit those downstream. Such polluters are unlikely to spend much on control unless pressured to do so.
19. cf. *The Ecologist* Vol. 1 No. 5. Goldsmith, 'The Cost of Pollution'.
20. For example, Colgate Palmolive and Coca Cola use this form of advertising. Nuclear power is also depicted as 'clean' yet it causes heat pollution, and nuclear stations destroy much shallow marine life in their proximity, in addition to creating dangers of radio-active waste and of nuclear explosions.
21. cf. Richard West, *River of Tears,* Earth Island, 1972. *The Rio Tinto Zinc Corporation Limited Anti-Report,* Counter Information Services 1972.
22. *Observer,* 30.1.72.
23. *The Rio Tinto Zinc Corporation Ltd. Anti-Report,* Counter Information Services 1972.

53

24. Caldwell, L. K., 1970.
25. Westergaard, J., 1966.
26. It could be that the limited evidence available is misleading—the absence of any campaign in Britain comparable to that for responsible management in America should not lead one necessarily to conclude that such a campaign is not needed.

Chapter Five: THE RESOLUTION OF CONFLICT

How far industry, public opinion and the various interest groups concerned have been important in influencing pollution legislation may be considered by referring to the literature on the issue, by analysing specific legislation, and by inquiring into the absence of legislation on other occasions. With this background, we will later consider the operation and basis of power as it influences pollution legislation, and the model of society this suggests.

The American Experience

It is suggested that a number of factors effectively influence governments to legislate on environmental matters but that in the absence of outside pressure, government, for reasons already stated, is unlikely to act. Davies concludes that there must be a significant demand from powerful interest groups before important action is taken, and Hagevik, from his study of decision making in air pollution control,[1] confirms that significant public policies emerge in the political process largely as a result of the conflict of group interests.

On occasion, public opinion too (in the form of a concerned majority of citizens demanding pollution control) has had an effect on policy. But public opinion is only seen to act in crisis situations, when an environmental disaster suddenly raises public awareness of pollution dangers and pressures government to act. Thus "Congress has reacted to crises, its responses, to a great degree being a function of the public's quickened and heightened awareness of all our problems resulting from the mass media".[2]

Support for this view comes from examination of a number of

Acts. In America the passage of the 1963 Clean Air Act was consequent upon an appreciation of the nature and dimensions of the air pollution problem following various crises and

> public pressure on the Federal Government to control air pollution increased greatly between 1963 and 1966 . . . concern both within the government and outside it was given dramatic force by a November 1966 pollution episode in New York City where a four-day inversion was estimated to have caused the death of eighty persons.[3]

By the end of 1969 the awareness of the public in America was such that there was a 'critical mass' of public opinion, sufficient to prompt the adoption of a national statement of policy for the environment in the form of State Law.

> The visible upsurge of public concern over environmental quality issues during the latter half of 1969 brought about the enactment of the National Environmental Policy Act with no extended debate or opposition that might have been expected to accompany the legislative course of so fundamental and novel a measure.[4]

Thus in America, pollution is now a vote-catching issue and in crisis situations carries a sufficient punch to overcome the influence of very well organised wealthy lobbies of industrialists. However, although public opinion, crises and interest group pressure may engender environmental legislation, the strength of this legislation depends largely on the effectiveness of various lobbies in mitigating the impact of a legislative measure where it affects them. Standard setting and compliance are heavily dependent on the political pressures applied to the government and on the political power available to the pollution control agencies. Subsequently we will suggest that pollution laws are so poorly enforced that industrialists face only ineffective legislation. Moreover, there is evidence that barriers to effective enforcement are built in at the legislative stage.

In 1968, Senate passed a Bill covering waste treatment, vessel and thermal pollution. The section on thermal pollution was designed to meet the basic problem that no Federal agency had the jurisdiction to prevent thermal pollution before it occurred. The sweeping language of the Bill led to strong opposition from the electrical industries and Chamber of Commerce who lobbied hard to defeat certain sections. Within the Executive Branch, the Corporation of Engineers feared the proposal could seriously interfere with its functions of licencing the dumping of dredging material, and the Atomic Energy Authority was even more vocal in its opposition, defending the interest of the nuclear power industry. The House of Representatives deleted any coverage of offshore and onshore facilities from the oil pollution section of the Bill; and it reduced the amount of liability for damage caused by oil discharges from vessels. "Overall the House version represented a set of significant concessions to polluting industries".[5]

In addition to the impact of vested interest groups exerting pressure on both sides,[6] the effective outcome of pressure for environmental legislation may depend upon the interests of government agencies. These may act on either side in the dispute depending upon who they represent, and the activities of the U.S. Department of Agriculture have already been described.

In this situation of conflicting interests, Lemert's analysis that "laws and rules produced in group interaction often reflect the values or norms of no group or persons but rather their dilemmas, compromises, expeditious adherence to procedures, and strictures of time and budget", may well prove fitting, although it is unsatisfactory in that it offers no means of predicting what sort of compromise will evolve. But one must accept that

> given the multitude of interest groups representing all shades of opinion on questions of pollution control, it is almost impossible to isolate the effects of interest groups per se. An administrator who appears to be acting totally independently may simply be anticipating the reactions of some group or set of groups in his decision.[7]

Nevertheless, in general terms, it may be said that industrial groups, often supported by the inertia of government, have been largely successful in handling legislative pressure, and that much of the existing legislation bears evidence of their impact in mitigating its effects upon them. It can further be said, following Davies, that an industry's political influence is generally relative to its size, its importance in the economy, and also probably the degree to which it is normally involved with government agencies.

Against the background of these arrangements of power must be placed the fluctuating impact of public opinion and conservationist pressure upon government to legislate on pollution control, which on occasion is given added support from those industries and interests which benefit from regulation of pollution. At present it can at least be stated that in America the current tide of conservationist pressure and popular concern with pollution has resulted in a situation where industry does not always have the upper hand. Thus, as a consequence of "political intrigue, the demands of local minorities, and pressure exerted by a majority",[8] Americans are likely to see the implementation of stringent new laws on the emission of car exhaust fumes, despite the delaying tactics of the automobile industry.

Nevertheless, this is evidence merely of an industry having to retrench, and it is not suggested that environmental consciousness has threatened in any fundamental way to loosen the grip of monopoly corporations over the political and moral climate of America. Nor is it suggested that existing pollution laws are either severely or effectively enforced, or that they cover the most dangerous forms of pollution.[9] Again it must be emphasised that public opinion is seen to act only when it is aware of a danger, and when that awareness prompts strong demands for action in times of obvious environmental crisis. Although it may be overtly successful, inasmuch as legislation results, in practical terms it may achieve little more than mild adjustment and image management on the part of industrial interests.[10]

Pollution Politics in Britain

In Britain, the environment has yet to become a genuine political issue of the importance, for example, of industrial relations or inflation. Some would argue that Britons have not been carried away by a 'wave of hysteria' such as that generated by the American media. More likely the British have not had as severe problems as Americans and it may be argued that the existing British public health, factory and environmental control machinery is more advanced than that of the United States.

Britain's relative inertia on the pollution issue may also be attributed to differences in the political system. The looseness of party ties in the U.S. makes it possible to persuade individual Congressmen to raise general questions of priorities and thus to represent environmental interests in a political fashion. In Britain, with its system of party discipline and party affiliation based largely on class and crude economic factors, this has not been possible except in the case of the Liberal Party whose effect appears to be minimal.

This is not to say that no action has been taken in Britain, or that public opinion has not been aroused, but Britain lacks a widespread environmental movement of organised proportions. The "Blueprint for Survival" called for a national movement, if need be to assume political status and contest the next general election. Such a movement shows little sign of emerging, and organised pressure on the government is often limited—in the absence of a general public outcry over specific events—to the efforts of largely voluntary conservationist organisations.

As in America, the British public has been stirred by crises. Only then, backed by strong public opinion, have the advocates of pollution control been able to neutralise the objections of those whose interests will be adversely affected by the proposed law. These have in the past included the bulk of British industry, which has been supported by the inertia of successive governments, to whom pollution control has seemed less than worthwhile and a rather costly venture which cannot be justified in terms of the short term aims of government, and of political expediency.[11]

The best illustration of this political situation and of legislation consequent upon a crisis, is the legislation which followed the London smog of 1952, in which four thousand lives were lost in the area of Greater London. This came after years of agitation by advocates of clean air who had been unable to get much public hearing until the arrival of that dramatic fog. Even in this case there was no immediate public outcry, perhaps because the extent of the fog's impact on health did not become apparent for some time. It took strenuous efforts by the National Smoke Abatement Society, together with a number of revealing and widely publicised reports on the effects of the smog, to stir up public feeling.[12] This forced the government at least into an appearance of activity, and in consequence the Beaver Committee was established to inquire into the causes of smoke pollution and to make recommendations upon which a subsequent Private Members Bill was based. Despite popular support and the feeling that something should be done, industry was reluctant to support the extra cost alone, but the Bill's sponsors resisted this demand for subsidy. Subsequently the Bill was withdrawn on the assurance that the government would bring its own Bill, but it is unlikely that the government would have taken action without pressure. Thus Mr. Smith noted how "Minister after Minister has answered questions in the House in the most complacent manner during the past ten years. We do not have to thank them, nor the Ministries, for taking resolute action".[13]

Unlike the originators of the former Bill, the government stressed consultation with industry and with the representatives of Local Authorities who claimed to support the broad principles of the Bill, subject to reservations. Many M.P.'s (mainly those from heavily polluted areas which had suffered most) were critical of the outcome. Dr. Summerskill recognised that although the Bill adopted the principal recommendations of the Beaver Committee,

> It has been hedged by so many savers and waivers as to render it abortive unless we exercise the greatest vigilance in its administration. It seems to have provided a mask through which the indifferent or incompetent producer of smoke can escape. Indeed, listening to the Parliamentary Secretary, it appeared to me almost as though the government had deliberately framed the measure so as to let industrialists escape . . . It is astonishing to think that a man can be charged with and convicted for a single physical assault but that, on the other hand he can assault the olfactory, visual and auditory senses of all his fellow townsmen for the whole of his life and still remain within the law.[14]

According to Mr Gerald Nabarro "the hand of the Federation of British Industries is writ large between the lines" and the shortcomings of the Bill were manifest. Mr. Batey, Superintendent Smoke Inspector for Sheffield, alleged that three wellnigh impregnable barriers to successful smoke prosecutions were raised by the Bill—inadequate regulations regarding lighting up, failure of apparatus, and unsuitable fuel.[15] The definition of 'any practicable means' of control in section 28 was found to be fatal for the purpose of the Act and no standards were laid down in the grit and dust provisions. If a firm installed grit arrestment apparatus and was not using it properly or allowing gross inefficiency in its use then suitable enforcement action was not possible.

In the face of mounting criticism, the Minister's attitude changed, and the Bill was given more teeth in committee, but the House failed to find a solution to the defence of using unsuitable fuel which Mr Nabarro considered would make it "nearly impossible to prosecute the recalcitrant industrialist who is still largely responsible for black and dark smoke".[16] Mr Winterbottom told the House of Commons that

> there are so many defences, so many limitations there is no clarity on the application of the Alkali Acts to many industries of Sheffield and district. Nearly all the industrialists, if they have the will, can use the Clean Air Bill to perpetuate nuisance . . . except the householder.[17]

The latter, devoid of the direct power and influence of industry, not organised in any lobby, and indeed often in favour of Clean Air Measures in the abstract, bore the burden of the Clean Air Act in adapting to smokeless fuels within Clean Air Zones.

The Act itself served to lull public fears and was effective in reducing the level of visible pollution as a consequence of its effect both on the householder and (despite its inadequacies) to an extent, on industry. It showed how the power of vested interest groups (in this case, industrial concerns) can reduce the impact of law, as it affects them, at the legislative stage—through the efforts of M.P.'s with vested industrial interests in reducing the effectiveness of law. While partially vindicating Lemert's claim that laws and rules often reflect compromise rather than the interests of any one group, the Act also illustrated that in the real world of inequality of power, compromise can become retrenchment of an interest by virtue of its organisational interpenetration of government, and that the limits of compromise lie within boundaries narrowly defined by those in power.

What the Act did not do was to deal with those invisible, less obviously detected pollutants which are frequently more dangerous than the visible ones.[18] As often happens, Parliament concerned itself with the most easily solved problem rather than with the most serious, and in this way could maintain its own legitimacy as a benevolent ruler.

More recent legislative evidence, indicative of a government's position and power on the pollution issue and of its resistance to any firmly enforced laws with severe penalties, is available in the Alkali Inspectorate Bill, 1973. This was an unsuccessful Private Members Bill which proposed a revision of the laws relating to atmospheric pollution. Its sponsor spoke of

> the mounting criticism, both nationally and in my constituency, of Her Majesty's Alkali Inspectorate [and of] a need for greater public accountability by the Inspectorate, with greater legal powers of enforcement being given to it in order that the public may have more knowledge of its work.[19]

Mr McBridge went on to demand an extension of the Alkali Inspectorate both in its members and in its powers to control emissions; to propose the deposit of performance bonds as tangible evidence of the genuine intention of industry to reduce pollution; and to outline his philosophy of enforcement.

> There must be no compromise with industry. The emission standards laid down in the Bill must be strictly adhered to . . . With modern atmospheric pollution it is criminal not to take stringent controls now to ensure as far as possible that all the toxic constituent agents are not poured unlimited into the air we breathe. This is detrimental and can have biochemical, toxicological, mutagenic and teratogenic effects, which are referred to in the Robens Report. More important still, they can have carcinogenic effects.[20]

Others noted that the present system, through the weakness and ineptitude of the Inspectorate, resulted in one important sector of polluters (industry), not having to meet its costs. In response to accusations of complacency, the Minister for Local Government and Development, on behalf of the government, denied that the Inspectorate was too familiar with industrialists, or that the present policy of co-operation was undesirable. He warned that the Bill would not receive government support in its present form and that "we would seek to maintain the present principle which I believe has worked well."[21]

The Minister's views illustrate that government is unlikely to act to create more severe or efficient laws on pollution unless pressurised into doing so. Such pressure must be very strong before it is successful, and in the absence of an obvious environmental crisis, there is every indication that the present system will, in essence, continue. Even where legislation is successfully invoked, the evidence on the working of the 1956 Clean Air Act suggests that a powerful industrial lobby will be capable of mitigating its effects by the use of provisos and the finding of loopholes whereby they can escape the intent of the Act. They may further be able to avoid its impact by relying on the leniency of the agencies entrusted with the enforcement of the laws. It is to these agencies that we turn next.

NOTES

1. Hagevik, G. K., 1970.
2. Oppenheim and Miller, 1970.
3. Davies, J. C., 1970.
4. Caldwell, 1970.
5. Davies, J. C., 1970.
6. c.f. The growing role of industries engaged in the making of pollution control equipment who lobby for more stringent legislation. In addition, other entire industries are even more politically significant and economically important than the control equipment producers. For example, the Natural Gas and Nuclear Power industries have been beneficiaries in the campaign against high sulphur coal.
7. Oppenheim and Miller, 1970.
8. *The Times,* 19.7.71.
9. See *infra* Chapter VII.
10. This may become clearer subsequently, when we consider the enforcement of pollution control legislation.
11. Government itself is involved in pollution making activities, for example, in controlling the nationalised industries.
12. For a fuller account of the activities and importance of the Smoke Abatement Society, see Sanderson, T. B. 'The Smoke Abatement Society and the Clean Air Act (1956)'. *Political Studies* 9–10, 1961–62.
13. *Hansard,* Vol. 536, p. 1452.
14. *Hansard,* Vol. 551, 10 April 1956.
15. Thus clause 1(3) prohibits dark smoke from chimneys, but then gives any factory owner the chance to plead successfully in defence that the fuel used was unsuitable.
16. *Hansard,* Vol. 551, 10 April 1956.
17. Ibid.
18. Sulphur Dioxide, for example, may be present in the air in sufficient quantities to be a health hazard (e.g., a lung irritant) yet remain invisible and undetectable by smell. Its regulation was raised but not legislated on during the passage of the Clean Air Act through parliament. This Act dealt predominantly only with black or dark smoke—

the obvious hazard which had visibly threatened the health of Londoners in the smog of 1952—but not necessarily the only or most dangerous threat to health.

19. *Hansard,* 11 May 1973, p. 943.
20. Ibid., p. 947–8.
21. Ibid., p. 972.

Chapter Six: THE ENFORCEMENT OF LEGISLATION

The existence of a rule does not automatically guarantee that it will be enforced. Since we cannot say that 'society' is harmed by every infraction and acts to restore the balance,[1] then the enforcement of such environmental legislation as exists, and the particular mode of enforcement, requires explanation as much as does the enactment of legislation—especially since industry's reaction to legislation is likely to be tempered by the likelihood and level of its enforcement.

One must consider Pearce's allegation that "the most economically significant crimes, those of the wealthy, are least publicised, investigated and punished with least stigma attached to known offenders". Certainly the pollution laws, like those outlawing a number of other business activities, differ from other laws in origin, philosophy, enforcement, and in the sanctions used to punish violators. As Quinney notes:

> legislative and administrative rulings against business practices tend to be lenient, favouring offenders of high social status . . . enforcement . . . relies primarily on specially created agencies rather than on the use of police and court procedures.

The Alkali Inspectorate, a special body, adjudges standards as a self-conceived partner of industry, not as an independent judge, and is caught between serving industry and serving the public. In this capacity it refuses to give the public information about air pollution standards agreed between the Inspectorate and companies, and allows companies themselves to take readings of air pollution at industrial premises and to send these on to the Inspectorate.

Penalties for violation of law are low, and persuasion and co-operation are preferred to prosecution, which is only used when a firm's attitude is felt to be bad (e.g., deliberately flaunting the law) rather than when it is experiencing genuine difficulties in complying with legislation for economic or technical reasons. The Chief Inspector in 1967 proudly reported that "only on three occasions in the last forty-seven years have court proceedings been brought".

A number of justifications have been offered for retaining the present policy of the Inspectorate rather than establishing upper limits enforceable through the law with heavy penalties for infringement. First, unlike 'ordinary' criminal activity such as theft or embezzlement, pollution is not a social evil whose eradication or reduction is without cost (apart from enforcement) for society. "The problem we now face is how to strike a balance between the benefits of a rising standard of living and its costs in terms of deterioration of the physical environment and quality of life".[2]

Secondly, it is alleged that to bring prosecution may not be a suitable way of controlling pollution. "Complicated legislation and standards usually require complicated and expensive means of supervision and inspection, with the danger that the system falls into disrespect when it cannot be enforced".[3] Other, possibly more effective, strategies to ensure compliance with legislation include persuasion, negotiation, economic sanction, international agreement and education.

Davies alleges that in America all pollution agencies are forced to recognise that legal proceedings against individual polluters can never be the chief goal of a compliance programme. "Formal hearings and court action consume an extraordinary amount of time and manpower. Furthermore, the courts are not experts on pollution and the outcome of court cases is always somewhat unpredictable". Yet this lack of expertise has never prevented the courts from concerning themselves with other activities—marriage, criminality, etc. Not until the courts have dealt with a form of behaviour for some time, can one expect predictability—but this must have been a 'teething trouble' with all new phenomena before the courts.

Whether the Alkali Inspectorate's justifications for its methods and philosophy are satisfactory or whether there is indeed bias in the administration of justice can be answered by examining the practical implications of its policies. The Inspectorate controls

66

industry using 'the best practicable means' to keep emissions to a minimum, and it is this phrase which exposes the disadvantage of exhortation over legislation. There is no doubt that in many cases the Alkali Act has worked well, and our air pollution policies are probably more effective than those of most other countries, nor is there any doubt that the Inspectorate's policy has earned the willing co-operation of many industries.[4]

> The measure of control the Inspectorate has achieved is better than any legislation that is more honoured in the breach—but there is still no substitute for putting standards on the statute book and providing the means for enforcing them.[5]

The policy of exhortation is always open to the charge that standards agreed on voluntarily, while better than nothing, are not nearly enough and sometimes protect industry more than the public.

The justification for the flexible standards is that "they can be altered to take account of improving technology and the demands of the public for a better environment".[6] But in recent years there have been a number of incidents in which the phrase 'best practicable means' has been found unsatisfactory. The phrase is taken to mean reasonably practical having regard to local conditions and circumstances, to the current technical knowledge, to compatibility with any duty imposed by law, and to the financial implications. Thus it takes into account the effect of control measures on the operation of the process and their cost.

The great danger of allowing economic factors to colour technical judgements is that an industry's arguments against incurring cleaning costs appear much more 'reasonable', not to say forceful, than the demands of those who have to breathe the air it pollutes. The decision on standards is also taken out of the hands of lawmakers and given to the Inspectorate (and very occasionally to local magistrates). According to Jeremy Bugler, the phrase 'best practicable means'

> reflects the economic convenience of industry. It is by no means adequate to prevent factories from passing on or externalising their air pollution costs to the local population in terms of soured amenity or higher laundry bills and lowered health.

An illustration of the practical working of the definition was seen in 1971 when the Swansea factory of United Carbon Black

Ltd. was blockaded by local people who were angry about the air pollution caused by the plant, yet the pollution standards of the factory had the approval of the Alkali Inspectorate in that the company was considered to be employing the 'best practicable means'. After the blockade, however, the company allocated large sums to improving its air emissions, which casts doubt on the adequacy of the enforced definition. Thus the Inspectorate has on occasion appeared as a bulwark to the polluter who can claim that his operation is within the law.

Another example of the tolerance the Inspectorate shows to industry is the much publicised case of heavy metal pollution around the plant of the Imperial Smelting Corporation (a Rio Tinto Zinc subsidiary) at Avonmouth, England. Scientists from Bristol University found levels of lead, zinc and cadmium in an area close to the smelter that were many hundreds of times higher than the limits laid down by the food hygiene regulations—and this after the factory was closed for some months when dangerously high levels of pollution were found in the blood of some smelter workers. Yet the Alkali Inspectorate was responsible for controlling the smelter's emissions.

Recent criticism of the Inspectorate also occurred when Leeds City Council requested the Secretary of State for the Environment to transfer to them full air pollution control powers over seven local factories and plants.[7] The Council is dissatisfied with the way the Inspectorate has controlled the plants, alleging that the Inspectorate has too small a staff, an ignorance of the cost of air pollution control, a too familiar relationship with polluters, and is not answerable to the local population which has to suffer the effects of pollution.

The Inspectorate's approach can be compared with the tough, uncompromising attitude in Philadelphia where "any substantial emission, even accidental or caused by breakdown (is treated) as a violation . . . The authorities believe that they will get a far better response by legal actions than they will by practising co-operation",[8] and, in Pennsylvania, factories are required to post 'performance bonds' from which penalties are levied if the factory overruns a pollution control schedule or fails to meet the standards.

In America the courts are more open to public suit and more flexible. Enforcement agencies have to cope with a tradition of unrestrained private enterprise, and the drive against industrial pollution started much later, for historical and economic reasons, than in Britain. For these reasons, the British Chief Alkali Inspector considers the American action both right and appropriate but not suitable for Britain. Nevertheless, as Bugler notes, if a large British company were required to 'make its excuses' to a court for a breakdown that caused pollution, then a dramatic improvement in the reliability of its plant would follow.[9] It is not enough to say that our courts are insufficiently flexible to allow for excuse making, for seemingly it would be a simple matter to reverse the onus of proof and make the defendant prove he had not been negligent in permitting pollution.

Thus it does not necessarily follow that strict enforcement of legislation would not be an effective means of control in Britain. The odd thing about the claim that a tough, uncompromising attitude would clog the law courts is that it is seldom if ever advanced as a reason for adopting a gentle approach to crimes against property.[10] Nor are the arguments of cost, difficulties of enforcement, lack of manpower, used to justify a policy of persuasion rather than strict enforcement against property crimes —perhaps because they attack the moral and economic base of propertied interest groups.

Bugler maintains that the environment is a public property immeasurably more valuable and irreplaceable than an individual's possessions. He alleges that objections to pollution policies that would be determined enough to carry through to the law courts if necessary, are founded on an inadequate appreciation of the social wrong of pollution.[11] Perhaps "what the offensive against pollution in Britain needs is not only new laws, agencies,[12] taxes and technologies but new attitudes".[13]

Pollution Control: Bias in the Administration of Justice?

If there is such a case for strict legislative control and prosecution, it is important to examine why this has not been effected, and why industry is at present in the comfortable position of being protected by the Inspectorate from public pressure for stricter standards. Is this, as Pearce claims, because these are the crimes of the wealthy whose influence results in ineffective laws?

We have already seen that legislation has in the past been rendered less effective by the efforts of the economically powerful, but the Inspectorate's methods and philosophy cannot be attributed entirely to this influence. Rather the historical development of the Inspectorate has also had an impact on its present position. Bugler shows that when the Inspectorate was first formed in 1863 it was often more knowledgeable about the air pollution problem than was industry itself. From this evolved the Inspectorate's "self-conceived role as an agency to help industry get on with the job, rather than as an air pollution control agency above it". This has resulted in the Inspectorate seeing "the industry's problems in close focus and the public's in a haze". What was an advance in 1863 may not be so now. Since that time the law has been amended in detail rather than in fundamentals and many contend that the time has come for revision of its basic concepts.

There is also another side to the philosophy and methods of the Inspectorate which can be revealed by examining the specific criminal activity of pollution in the particular socio-historical context in which it occurs—"we must focus on the effects of different kinds of crime and thereby explain why the State wishes to prosecute certain offences and not others".[14] Pollution control equipment is often sophisticated and expensive and on some occasions there is no satisfactory technology to deal with the problem. Some, generally smaller, firms could not reduce their pollution to a strict statutory standard and survive. Thus in some circumstances they are given up to ten years to improve their standards, and in any case are only prosecuted when their attitude is considered unsatisfactory. In cases of severe financial difficulty the chances of pressure or prosecution by the Inspectorate are remote.

This is in keeping with the predictions of Marx on the Factory Acts.

> If it were made obligatory to provide the proper space for each workman in every workshop, thousands of small employers would at one fell swoop, be expropriated directly! The very root of the capitalist mode of production, i.e. the self expansion of all capital, large or small, by the 'fair' purchase and con-

sumption of labour power, would be attacked. Factory legislation is, therefore, brought to deadlock before those five hundred cubic feet of breathing space . . . the Factory inspectors . . . harp over and over again, upon the necessity of those five hundred feet and upon the impossibility of wringing them out of capital.[15]

Thus the philosophy of the Inspectorate operates in the interests of capitalism. In particular, it protects the smaller capitalists from the economic consequences of their activities; pollution costs are thereby not borne by those who cause pollution or by the purchasers of their products, but are borne instead by the victims of pollution.

Another possible philosophy of enforcement is suggested by the emphasis placed by the Alkali Inspectorate on the 'attitude' of industry, which is regarded as even more important than the level of pollution.[16] It may be that the absence of any real power over industry forces the Inspectorate into a position whereby it is more concerned with the firm's image management than with its harm to the environment. Thus, where a firm appears to be doing something about pollution, the Inspectorate can maintain its legitimacy as an agent of a benevolent capitalist state, and the corporate managers can maintain the appearance of social responsibility.

This perspective—that the Inspectorate is not over-concerned with the level of the firm's pollution—is given some support by the way activities are conducted. Firms are allowed to take their own readings of pollution levels and then report these to the Inspectorate, and occasions have been documented when a firm has been given prior warning that the Inspectorate will be arriving.[17]

Nevertheless, the power of the Alkali Inspectorate is ostensibly in its own hands—it alone interprets what are 'the best practicable means' of limiting pollution and it could, if necessary, force firms to close down. What constrains it from doing so may be the apparent disfunctionality of making criminals of those whose activities benefit the economy of the State, and its appreciation (reinforced by its origins and development) of the effects of strict enforcement on capitalism. This philosophy of enforcement reflects and maintains the interests of the politically and economically powerful, capitalist class.

Nevertheless, enforcement activity cannot be seen purely in a class/power model. More severe sanctions against industrial polluters would cause consequent unemployment if small capitalists were forced out of business. The policy of the Alkali Inspectorate involves a direct bias in the administration of justice in favour of the powerful only in so far as one regards the possibility of reducing the quality and length of the lives of others as more important than fuller employment—and the proprietary rights of smaller capitalists. Effectively the choice is between employment and health.

This choice however, need only be made within a capitalist society. The ultimate goal of capitalism being the accumulation of capital and making of profit, industry must make a profit to survive. In a socialist economy, where the main goal is the satisfaction of human needs, a firm might serve the public better by being pollution-free than by making a profit.

Local Authority Control

Control of industrial air pollution in Britain is shared between local and central government and therefore concerns not only the Alkali Inspectorate (though this is the most important body), but also Public Health Inspectors of Local Authorities. The former are responsible for some 1700 registered premises covering about 3,000 scheduled processes, whereas the latter, administering the Clean Air Acts and associated legislation, are responsible for a wide range of industrial and fuel using processes in about 300,000 commercial and industrial premises in England and Wales.

Their relationship with industry is not as sympathetic as that of the Alkali Inspectorate (which makes the opposition of industry to the 1956 Clean Air Act understandable). The Public Health Inspectorate has made much progress and there has been a significant reduction of smoke in the last ten years, although it is still concerned about the level of grit, dust, gas and odour emissions.[18]

In some circumstances, Health Inspectors labour under the same difficulties of conflicting interests as do the Alkali Inspectorate. Throughout Britain, Local Authorities are unwilling to pressurise industries too much for fear they will go elsewhere, and on a national level, government is concerned that pollution control will mean more expensive products and a consequent disadvantage in international trading.

NOTES

1. Differences in the ability to make rules and apply them are essentially power differentials—those groups whose social position gives them the instruments of power are best able to enforce their rules—but are only likely to do so if it serves their interests.
2. Royal Commission on Environmental Pollution 1971.
3. The Chief Inspector of Alkali.
4. The Royal Commission on Environmental Pollution stressed that "in the abatement of pollution there is already a close and constructive co-operation which has led to impressive improvement of the environment of Britain in the last two decades".
5. R. Allen, *The Ecologist,* Vol. 1. No. 12.
6. F. E. Ireland, Chief Inspector of Alkali.
7. *Observer,* 24.12.72.
8. Bugler, J., 1972.
9. This, indeed, has been proposed by the Alkali Inspectorate Bill, 1973 but is rejected by government.
10. Once a new and more rigorous standard was established, little more prosecution would be needed than is occasioned by the obligation to pay taxes.
11. Ball and Freidman claim that there is no sharp classification into 'economic crimes' which can be marked off from other offences with respect to morality. They conclude that the argument that business crimes are not immoral is circular. The reason why traditional categories of crime are regarded as immoral is precisely that they have long been included in the traditional categories of crime. The 'business offences' are not perceived as immoral because they have not been included among the traditional crimes, and they have not been included among these because they are not immoral.

    In the most recent of the rare pollution cases that go to court, one member of the House of Lords at least, adopted traditional definitions. Viscount Dilhorne in Alphacell v. Woodward (*Times* 4th May 1972), thought that polluting rivers fell into the category of acts not criminal in any real sense but merely contrary to public policy.
12. The Robens report on Safety and Health at Work recommends that the existing separate safety and health inspectorates should be amalgamated to form a unified service.
13. Bugler, J., 1972.

14. Pearce, F., 1973.
15. Marx, K., *Capital.* New York. International Publishers. Vol. 1. p. 482.
16. This is similar to the attitude to the Factory Acts which W. G. Carson has analysed in similar fashion. "It was when a firm's previous history was interpreted as an indication of its unsatisfactory attitudes rather than its adverse economic position or otherwise extenuating circumstances that severe enforcement was likely to occur". *B.J.C.* 10 1970.
17. e.g., *Sunday Times Magazine,* 2.4.72.
18. Stated opinion of R. Johnson, Secretary, Association of Public Health Inspectors.

Chapter Seven: THE POLITICS OF POLLUTION—
CONSENSUS OR CONFLICT?

The enactment and enforcement of legislation can be seen either as the result of a consensus, as a consequence of competing interest groups, but within a value-neutral framework, or as the consequence of power relationships in which "the system of representation in the corridors of power will operate to the benefit of some interest groups and to the disadvantage of others".[1] Some sympathy has been expressed with the latter position while recognising that all laws lie on a continuum between consensus and conflict. It is the present aim, utilising the conclusions of previous chapters, to place pollution legislation (and the lack of it) somewhere on that continuum, and to explain the laws that exist and their enforcement, in terms of a model of society and of law creation.

American Politics: The Inadequacy of Pluralism

First, we can consider how far the evidence fits the conventional view of the formal democratic system of power as operating within a balancing society in which no unit of power is strong enough to do more than edge forward a bit at a time, in compromised counterbalance with other such forces. This analysis, combined with the doctrine of public opinion, would suggest a pluralistic consensus model of society and would deny that pollution laws are produced by a politically and economically powerful minority.

Such a model must be rejected for two reasons. First, the role that interest groups have played in influencing pollution legislation reveals not a plurality of groups operating within a balancing

75

society, but a small number of unequally powerful interests dominating the legislative struggle to the cost of their opponents —a point to which we will return later. Second, the orthodox doctrine of public opinion embodied in the pluralistic consensus model of society, is that the 'general will' of the population becomes enacted in legislation. But this view, despite its contemporary exponents,[2] is difficult to reconcile with specific features of the social structure, and with the facts of pollution legislation.

We have already argued that no working consensus exists on the extent to which pollution should be controlled, so the most that public opinion can claim to represent is the views of a majority of the population, and even such a limited concept of public opinion must become increasingly inadequate as society becomes more of a 'mass' than a public.[3] This structural transformation is described by Mills as follows:

> In the primary public the competition of opinions goes on between people holding views in the service of their interests and their reasoning. But in the mass society of media markets, competition, if any, goes on between the manipulators with their mass media on the one hand, and the people receiving their propaganda on the other.

Public opinion thus only acts when the public becomes aware of a problem. It is influenced by political leadership, by the public advertising and selling efforts of corporations, and by those who control the media.

Under such conditions the influence of public opinion (or at least of different groups within a pluralist society) upon legislation may depend increasingly upon the importance of voluntary associations as genuine instruments of the public. But these are declining and following C. Wright Mills' analysis of the structure of American society, we note that not only have the institutions of power become large scale and inaccessibly centralised, but within them political questions have been defused of their visible political content and have been presented as administrative or technical questions (for example the depoliticisation of the criminal question and its redefinition as a welfare problem), and it is within this framework that public organisation has waned.

> Mass democracy means the struggle of powerful and large-scale interest groups and associations, which stand between the big

76

decisions that are made by state, corporation, army, and the will of the individual citizen as a member of the public. Since these middle-level associations are the citizen's major link with decisions, his relation to them is of decisive importance, for it is only through them that he exercises such power as he may have.

However, at a time when the top of American society is becoming increasingly unified and powerful, the middle levels are a

drifting set of stalemated, balancing forces: the middle does not link the bottom with the top. The bottom of this society is politically fragmented, and even as a passive fact, increasingly powerless. At the bottom there is emerging a mass society.

At the bottom in America, the people belong to no co-ordinated associations, to no groups capable of impressing their interests on the powerful. Even if the working class have strong feelings about pollution (which at the moment seems unlikely) they would have insufficient means or power to express them, except amid a multitude of other interests during the election process.

Thus the limited impact of public opinion on legislation becomes explicable in terms of Mills' analysis. As we noted previously, it is only in crisis situations that the general public have been a force exerting strong pressure on government. Only when large numbers of people die in a short time and this can be attributed directly to the effects of pollution (e.g. the Donata and London 'killer' smogs) does almost everyone demand legislation in a politically effective manner. Only then, when government must appear to act in order to maintain its legitimacy as guardian of 'society's interests',[4] does public opinion force government action.

Even then, as we have shown, the impact of vested interest groups is strong in mitigating the force of that legislation as it affects them. Moreover, it is apparent that some groups are more powerful than others. From the significant lack of pollution laws on specific environmental dangers,[5] from the weakness both of existing legislation and its enforcement, from the evidence we have cited of specific legislation and from various studies, we suggest that the state of legislation not only favours, but has been strongly influenced by, powerful industrial and governmental forces whose economic base is one of financial and industrial capital. Conversely, there is little evidence of conservationists, moral entrepreneurs or those involved in 'expressive politics' succeeding in having their views implemented in legislation. This suggests that we live not in a balanced society, but in a society composed of unequal conflicting groups in which the units of power that count are "few in number and weighty beyond comparison with the dispersed groups on the middle and lower levels of the power structure".[6]

These units may be seen, following Kolko, to consist of men committed to the capitalist status quo:

> What is absolutely essential to any understanding of power in America, and the purpose of it, is that . . . all men at the top in any sector of the power structure have been in agreement on the desirability of preserving essentially the existing distribution of wealth and income in the United States. They have, in brief, favoured the maintenance of a capitalist society, and it is within this absolute class criteria that they have applied their power.

This analysis of the nature of power, as applied to the issue of pollution legislation, would explain the inability of those at the bottom, or in the middle levels of society (e.g. various conservation groups, local county and state groups) to have their views implemented in legislation. It would explain why the state of pollution legislation represents the interests of industralists and financial capitalists and why the evidence indicates their success, both in resisting legislation and in mitigating its effects on those occasions when environmental crisis forces it upon them. It would also deny that America is a balanced, pluralist society.

A further inadequacy of the pluralist model is that it assumes that the units in the balance are independent of each other. But we should consider how far these various formally separate groups are in fact not distinct and competing interests, but broadly similar. If this is so, they cannot be seen as elements of a free and open balance.

In America, according to Mills, the major vested interests often compete less with one another in their effort to promote their several interests, than they coincide, and indeed come together under the umbrella of government. The power elite is shaped by the coincidence of interest among economic, military and political organisations, and its unity is maintained by the similarity of origin and outlook, and the social and personal intermingling of the top circles from each of these dominant hierarchies.

The interaction of government and industry is described by Kolko, who observes that there has been no sustained clash between any federal agency in existence, or created during this century, and the industry it nominally regulates. But more important, he maintains, is

> power's essential structure and purpose which, on the economic and political level, has always been the preservation and extension of American capitalism as a total system combining the administration of economic as well as political sectors, each reinforcing the needs of the other as a political economy.

These views, although substantiated by reference to specific legislation, must be tempered with some observations about recent developments in America. These developments, while not denying the substantial importance of the rulers of American capitalism in controlling legislation, nevertheless suggest that no one group has a stranglehold on power. Thus stringent controls are being forced upon a number of strong vested interests—the automobile companies being the most recent example. Although such laws may be functional to industry (which might otherwise suffer a total closedown), there is no indication that the corporate heads and managers see the situation in this way—they have been strongly and bitterly opposed to pollution control.

Thus an analysis based on a monolithic conception of power cannot be completely accepted. The existence of legislation against the interests of large industries suggests that no one group has a monopoly of power, that the middle range groups have more political significance than Mills attributes to them, that laws produced by group interaction are often a result of compromise rather than of any outright victory of any one group, and that the impact of pollution as a vote-catching issue has on occasion influenced decisions.

Nevertheless, any measures for control, proposed or adopted, are always conditioned by the initial assumption that entrenched rights of private ownership and private profit are sacrosanct.[7] As Westergaard notes, in so far as various interests and pressure groups participate in, or make their voices heard in the making of decisions and the formulation of policies, they do so only within this initial assumption. Such is the extent of 'pluralism'.

The nature of power in Britain, for a number of reasons, differs from that in America. In Britain, the predominant power of private capital has been challenged by the labour movement, whose opposition finds institutional expression in the political as well as the industrial field. A tradition of social democracy—class based parties subject to some accountability to their constituencies—has been established.

This is in contrast to the American political structure, which may be explained, partly at least, by the absence of any similar politically independent working class movement. The prevailing American ideology, emphasising independence, individualistic striving, competitive progress and mobility, finds expression in a theory of political structure, where politics are more individualistic, party ties weaker than in Britain, and equality of opportunity is said to allow anyone with ability to rise to the top.[8]

In Britain, pressure group activities, to gain success, must act largely through the two-party system, either through the Conservative Party—representative of the managers, the capitalists, the petty bourgeoisie and the upwardly mobile middle class—or the Labour Party—traditionally incorporating the Trade Unions, the white working class and perhaps the Left intelligentsia. Whether or not this system is more democratic, more in line with the pluralistic interpretation of the distribution of power as governed by 'checks and balances', than the American system may be seen by examining the interests involved in the politics of pollution in Britain, and their relative success (in terms of policies and decisions implemented in legislation). This may reveal not only at what point between them the balance has been struck, but also reveal whether they operate within a pluralistic or conflict model of society.

Three distinct positions have been taken in relation to the environment. The most radical position claims that the capitalist market economy has not, and will not, be able to deal with the environmental problems we are facing, because its ethos of exploitation for individual gain is fundamentally incompatible with the ethos of environmental protection.[9] Groups and individuals taking this or a similar view include individual moral entrepreneurs such as Paul Ehrlich, materially disinterested

80

groups of conservationists (Friends of the Earth, the Conservation Society), *The Ecologist* magazine, the British Society for Social Responsibility in Science, and new 'deviant' groups involved in what Gouldner terms "Modern Psychedelic Romanticism" and expressive politics. It is largely from amongst these individuals and groups that the initial awareness of pollution as a 'social problem' emerged. Such groups have in common a conspicuous lack of a propertied interest in environmental politics. If their motives are mixed in other respects, they come together on this, which may be significant in explaining the resolution of legislative conflict.

At the other extreme are those who see pollution as a minor problem and distraction from the major issues that society should be involved with. As some of the problems of pollution become increasingly obvious and inescapable, this group is diminishing. In the past it has been represented predominantly by government (for reasons already stated), by an industrial lobby with strong vested interests in opposing control, and in America by those government departments representative of industrial interests. Both government and industry are now changing their position, and although Goldsmith takes it as axiomatic that they will spend as little on pollution control as they can get away with, political and economic necessity [10] are leading both to concern themselves with the problem. Specifically, pollution now has vote-catching potential,[11] and government must appear to act to safeguard the health of its citizens in order to maintain its legitimacy. At the same time, certain parts of industry are coming to realise that their long term aims may be better served by limiting their present level of pollution, and sufficient pressure exerted on industrialists may also force them to present an image of social responsibility.

But both government and industry, when they act, are likely to do so by a mild interference with the present system, rather than by any radical reversal of our allegedly destructive growth technology. The radical solution of *The Ecologist* would produce a shrinking tax base, falling revenues, higher costs, shrinking markets, lower G.N.P.—all results in antithesis to the present aims and policies of government.

Industry is also committed to the political and economic status quo—to an economic system in which it must make a profit to survive—and it too will resist all legal measures contrary to this aim. Thus both will try to solve the problems of pollution within existing aims and policies. Their position is well represented in Lord Robens' warning that to decry economic development in general in order to eliminate some of its otherwise preventable by-products, is to risk destroying the basis on which ultimately both amenity and natural achievement depend.[12]

Other groups favouring this approach have included groups of scientists involved in status politics, and what Wright Mills calls groups of the middle levels of American society (regional, state and local interests with limited demands for subsidies, reduced taxation etc.). But in Britain the most significant among those who resist demands for any radical reversal of present policies have been industrial and financial capitalists and members of both major British political parties. It seems that the fundamental distinction between those who oppose strict pollution control, and those who demand it, is one of property—and what defines a capitalist society is its property system.[13]

With this in mind, the point at which the balance between competing interests has been struck, must be examined. This cannot be confined merely to establishing the outcome of conflict between expressly formulated alternative policies and views, for as Westergaard notes,

> these proposals themselves have to be formulated within the limits of a 'realistic' tactical appraisal of the likely outcome, and within the limits of the institutionalisation of conflict which is the essence of contemporary politics. Such institutionalisation means that conflict is regulated through a series of compromises which define, not only the means and procedures of conflict, but also the area of conflict at any given time.

In Britain, legislation on the environment has been limited. The Clean Air Act, 1956, was a major piece of legislation, the law relating to dumping of toxic materials has recently been tightened [14]—again after a flurry of press activity—but these forms of pollution are neither different in kind from, nor more serious than, many others that go unlegislated. Professor Bryce-Smith remains sceptical of any improvement in the air, in health terms, resulting from the 1956 Clean Air Act,[15] and notes that there is still no statutory limit on the level of any air pollutant in our cities. Levels of asbestos bodies and heavy metals particularly give rise to concern, and events in Southwark [16] and Avonmouth in 1972, and on the Isle of Dogs the previous year, indicate that the present system of controlling contamination around lead works is wholly inadequate.[17]

Even the laws that exist have not been accompanied by a policy of strict control and enforcement, nor, often, have their provisions been adequate to fulfil their intended purposes, as we saw in the case of the 1956 Clean Air Act. Despite this, we are unlikely to see any substantial change in the system because more inspectors, wider and more flexible powers, heavy penalties that are regularly enforced, are clearly not steps envisaged by either the government [18] or the Alkali Inspectorate.

We have shown that the policy of the Inspectorate in requiring industry to control pollution levels by the 'best practicable means' reflects the economic convenience of industry,[19] and further that the philosophy of the Inspectorate operates in the interests of capitalism. Thus, since strict enforcement of more severe legislation would attack the very root of capitalism (profit making and the self-expansion of capital, large and small), then any compromise between alternative policies and views is always struck within an area which does not threaten these interests.

That only this small span of the full range of alternatives is seriously considered, is a consequence of the political power structure in Britain, where power can be seen as held largely by

a small homogenous elite of wealth and private corporate property—politically entrenched in the leadership of the Conservative Party; strongly represented in, or linked with, a variety of influential public and private bodies, assured of the general support of the press, its members sharing for a large part a common exclusive educational background, and united by fairly close ties of kinship and everyday association . . . it is an elite which [has] its economic base of financial and industrial capital.[20]

This industrial and government grouping, with similar material interests in resisting pollution control, is challenged significantly only by the labour movement. Other channels of opposition tend either to be ineffective or to be absorbed into the Labour Party, through which the only effective opposition can be mounted in the long run.

The reason for the ineffectiveness of radical demands for

83

environmental control becomes explicable within this structure. They are unable to integrate themselves within the Labour Party because the latter is now a party of social improvement within the capitalist system,[21] and because it is faced with many of the same problems as a Conservative Government and uses several similar policies to solve those problems. The generation of extra wealth which will be preferentially distributed to the poorer members of society, continues to be defended as the only politically feasible way of closing the gap between rich and poor in this country, and continued even faster growth, remains a plank of both Conservative and Labour Party policy. Even if Labour adopted a radical environmental policy (which seems particularly unlikely in view of the short term threat to employment this would create), it would be unlikely to be implemented in legislation. Although the rise of labour has clearly imposed restraints upon the exercise of power by the primary elite, "the institutionalised compromise which characterises the scene of political conflict has been drawn up at a point which still predominantly favours the interests of capital".[22]

Conflict or Pluralism?

In order to maintain a pluralistic model of society, it is necessary to establish that power is scattered among a diversity of interests, none of which is dominant, and among which power is balanced. This pluralistic model also assumes that the units in the balance are independent of each other—for otherwise they cannot be seen as elements of a free and open balance.

Westergaard has shown the inadequacy of such an interpretation. Although those at the bottom of the social scale have the means of impressing their views on those in power (by trade unions, by constituency parties), it has been shown that at the top there is a clustering of major sources of pressure, that the units at the top are not distinct and competing but broadly similar (and are based on class, property, and wealth), and that any group whose aims cannot be absorbed into the policies of one of the two major political parties, has no chance of having them implemented in legislation. Any compromise solution to conflict is always resolved, not from within the full range of alternatives which represent the interests of the contending groups, but within a narrower span which favours the interests of capital.

Groups involved in the politics of pollution are not operating in a balanced pluralistic society in which power is distributed among a variety of groups whose relative strengths are peacefully resolved in the value-neutral arena of the legislature. Rather, "the processes by which struggle for state power is carried out are warped in favour of one contending group or another".[23] The value-free model of the state must be rejected because the success of the various parties to the bargaining over legislation is governed by the rules and structure of the political system. These themselves, as normative, cannot be value-free. Just as a government based on checks and balances is, by that very fact, a weapon in the hands of those who would oppose extensive government intervention in the economy, so also is a two-party system a weapon in the hands of those who oppose measures which cannot be absorbed into the policies of those parties. Since, too, within that system, the balance of power favours a dominant class (the economic base of whose power lies in rights of private corporate property), it may be suggested that rather than representing the framework within which competing pressures jockey for position and make politics, the government itself embodies specific interests and policies, on which the opposition of labour has imposed only limited restraints.

If society does not rest on value consensus but is itself rent by value conflicts between the various special interest groups in the community, if power is not scattered among these diverse interests so that they are balanced and independent, if conflict is resolved only within a narrow span of the full range of alternatives, and if the State is not a value-free framework to moderate and contain the struggle, then the model of society that is left is one of conflict, and

> the State and its vast machinery for creating myth and symbol, for inspiring support, even from those whose interests are most injured by its activity, and in the final analysis, its monopoly of the means of violence and coercion, is itself the principle weapon and main prize in the struggle.[24]

Within this model, we have located power as lying within a

dominant capitalist group whose interests are best served by avoiding any radical reorganisation of present aims and policies. Thus it is understandable that neither industry nor government and its agencies have been prominent among those arousing concern about atmospheric pollutants. It is equally unsurprising that even when the government and local agencies responsible for the prevention of public poisoning have become aware of the dangers, the inadequacies of the present system have not necessarily been put right.[25]

The lack of statutory limit on any atmospheric pollutant in Britain implies that legislation is unlikely to be enacted in the absence of pressure on government. How then, do we account for the legislation that exists? How do we incorporate it within the conflict power model which we have specified?[26] Does the existence of such legislation, seemingly placing limitations on the behaviour of the powerful, suggest that power does not rest predominantly within the dominant capitalist class? Examination of the forces of pressure on the dominant class, and of its results, lends support rather than doubt to our proposed model.

Pressure for legislation has come from two sources—interest group activity and public opinion. Pressure groups have been predominantly groups with no material interest in pollution control and, in a society where power rests on property interests, they have been unable to enforce their demands in legislation. Their warnings are met by a denial that the environment is being seriously threatened, and their views are treated as exaggerated or hysterical.

Government success in creating this impression has been aided by a process which Gouldner calls 'normalised repression'. He writes:

> the power to enforce moral claims is never equally distributed. The level at which moral default comes to be stabilised is, in large part, determined by the relative power of the groups involved . . . the powerful can conventionalise their moral defaults. As their moral failure becomes customary and expected, this itself becomes another justification for giving the subordinate group less than it might theoretically claim under the group's common values. It becomes, in short, normalised repression.

Just as power can shape the definition of what is moral, so, aided by its ability to control the media, it can shape the definition of what is dangerous, and harmful. Moral defaults become rationalised in such terms as "where there's muck there's brass", "firms have to make a profit", and the interests of the powerful come to be represented as the interests of society.

Action has only been taken when pressure group activity has been accompanied by a strong popular demand for environmental protection, but it is only when pollutants are easily detected and obviously harmful that the public becomes aware of them—public opinion is more acted on than acting. Silence from the government may lead the public to believe that the problem is solved when visible pollutants vanish, whereas in reality the most dangerous pollutants remain much as before. This misleading impression may be further reinforced by the image management activities of industry and government.[27]

Even the laws that have resulted (although enacted in response to public opinion) are often so weak as to be virtually unenforceable, and even if enforceable, are systematically under-enforced by the Alkali Inspectorate. Thus the pollution laws may be of that class which Pearce claims serve

> to dramatise an imaginary social order and hence legitimate the economic structure in terms of a misleading portrayal of its nature. They further appear to vindicate the claim that the State is neutral, in that it seems that every group, no matter how powerful, is subject to the will of the majority.

So it can be seen that the emergence of pollution laws seemingly in antithesis to the interests of the powerful, while appeasing 'public opinion', in no way alter the structure of power, nor do they significantly harm powerful interests.

The Future

There is every indication that this situation will continue until changes are experienced in the political system and its means of control. At present the means to power are influenced strongly by the two-party system, the specific interests of which [28] militate against some more general interest in the preservation of the environment.

Any radical change in present policies would depend on the break-up of traditional constituencies and the emergence of a third force which is not densely built into a narrow, particularist political and social structure, and which can overcome those who represent the issue as an alternative between environment and unemployment. Such a force has yet to emerge.

NOTES

1. Chambliss and Seidman, 1971.
2. Thus, for example, Max Nicholson (1970) claims that it is now possible for ordinary people directly to influence Congress and the White House. If so then "the entire character of the American conservation movement as mainly a tournament between the chosen champions of battling interests, could be altered".
3. This occurs according to Mills, when
    (a) Fewer people express opinions than receive them.
    (b) The communications that prevail are so organised that it is difficult or impossible for the individual to answer back immediately with any effect.
    (c) The realisation of opinion in action is controlled by authorities who organise and control the channels of such action.
    (d) The means to action cannot be separated from institutions.
4. Government seeks its legitimation through the claim that it is affected with "a public interest rather than with a special limited set of goals. Much of the effective acceptance of government as legitimate rests upon the suggestion that it is representative of the total society". Sutton.
5. See infra.
6. Mills, C. W., 1956. On the question of the relative power of middle and lower levels, one need only refer to the concentration of financial wealth as some index of concentration of power. 1% of the United States population owns 80% of the corporate wealth. c.f. G. Kolko, *Wealth and Power in America*, Praeger 1962. M. Zeitlin (ed) *American Society Inc.*, Markham, 1970.
7. For example, industry, when faced with demands for pollution control, frequently pleads that it cannot afford to implement them. This is accepted as a legitimate and valid argument. Pearce asks "what price human life, compared to economic profit?"
8. In practice, as Wright Mills shows, America "is now in considerable part more a formal democracy than a democratic social structure, and even the formal political mechanics are weak".

9. The present system is said to function for the benefit of certain groups at the expense of others, and for those now living at the expense of generations to come. This analysis suggests that a social system is needed in which the purpose of production and economic activity is not profit but the satisfaction of genuine needs, and in which decisions to undertake an activity are made not simply after allowing for unavoidable costs to the entrepreneurs, but only when all environmental and social effects have been assessed.

10. The level of pollution is becoming so bad in certain places, or will be so before long, that industrial activities can no longer be continued. In such circumstances, pollution control becomes imperative.

    Thus D.D.T. was banned for two years in Sweden only when herrings were found to contain higher than permissible levels of the poison, which rendered them unsaleable. In Britain the Clean Air Act was passed only after 3,000 people had died from the effects of smog in the winter of 1952, and the experience in Italy where industry has run out of usable water, has already been documented.

11. At present, however, the moral climate (asserting an attack on inflation, emphasising individualism, taking up international monetary crises) works against a collective politics of concern of the kind implied by environmentalism.

12. Thus Mr Eldon Griffiths, the Under-Secretary at the Department of the Environment, has firmly rejected the argument that economic growth should be held back to safeguard the environment from pollution.

    Replying to the debate on the environment, he said "The right course in my view will more and more have to do with the use of increasing resources to build quietness into engines, to pour less and less toxic effluent into our rivers and the sea, and to pay the price—and it will be a high one—of clearing up our mess as we go along". *Guardian* 12.10.72.

13. The Labour Party cannot be regarded as an exception to this distinction for, as Miliband and others have argued, it has become a party of social improvement within the capitalist system, rather than one committed to opposing capitalism under Clause 4 of its 1918 Constitution.

14. The Deposit of Poisonous Wastes Act, 1972, provides a maximum fine on summary conviction of £400 or up to six months' imprisonment, or both. In a higher court, the maximum penalty is five years' jail or a fine, or both.

15. The Act is concerned mainly with smoke, grit and dust, and does nothing to reduce emissions of sulphur dioxide, a powerful lung irritant, the level of which correlates closely with the death rate in London smogs. Bryce-Smith notes that some central areas of London now have sulphur dioxide levels high enough to produce increased hospital admissions and absenteeism from work, even when smoke levels are low.

16. The *Guardian*, 18.11.72.

17. Lead is a nerve and brain poison. In its developing phase the central nervous system may be particularly sensitive. A report on adult poisoning in the British Journal of Industrial Medicine confirms not only that neural and behavioural damage may precede overt signs of lead

poisoning but that the extent of nervous system damage may be independent of other symptoms. This is a very serious finding which, taken in conjunction with U.S. studies of behavioural abnormality in children exposed to urban levels of lead no greater than those common in British and European cities, calls for a complete reappraisal of prevailing assessments of the importance of lead as a public hazard.

18. See *Hansard* 11.5.73, p. 972.

19. Examination has revealed the Inspectorate's justifications for its policies to be inadequate, and recent incidents alone—R.T.Z., Carbon Black, Portland Cement—are sufficient to suggest that the Inspectorate is not working satisfactorily.

In addition to individual failures to act, the government has given itself no machinery for looking at environmental problems as a whole, preferring instead to deal with its many aspects as if they were self-contained analytic units.

Further we should ask why there are as yet no permanent testing teams with a reserve right of entry onto polluters premises (as the 1973 Bill proposes), why the Inspectorate has no research department to determine appropriate standards, why there is no accounts department to assess the financial capacity of industry to provide air pollution equipment, and to provide information about the financial capacity of a company to install the equipment the Inspectorate would regard as necessary.

20. Westergaard, J., 1966.

21. From the late 1940's on, when the Labour Party opted for 'consolidation' and retreated from reformism, then theoretically, as well as practicably, it ceased to oppose capitalism. In relation to the Conservatives, it remains to the left, but in any other perspective it is a party of the modified status quo able to provide an alternative government, but not an alternative social order. The Labour leaders are firmly rooted within the present system, and differences between Conservatives and Labour concern the management of a system whose basic features both sets of leaders accept and support. The control by the leaders of the party apparatus places them in an excellent position to ward off any substantial challenge from the left, and they may well believe that to adopt a radical environmental policy would be misguided, irrelevant, and perhaps even electorally self-defeating.

Nor must we assume that the radical left, within, or outside the Labour Party, would want a 'radical' environment policy. They have, in general, seen the issue simplistically, as an ideological diversion from the crisis in capitalism.

22. Westergaard, J., 1966.

23. Chambliss and Seidman, 1971.

24. Ibid.

25. A good example is lead, known to be a dangerous pollutant, yet inadequately controlled. Both politically and industrially, lead contamination is a sensitive subject, for it involves major commitments and investments. It would be politically convenient for government through its public health agencies to give the impression that once the local 'hot spots' have been cleared up then the problem will go away, but evidence suggests very strongly that high lead levels are to be found in children in all sectors of the urban population, not only around the lead works.

A recent report (*Which* magazine, April 1973) also suggested that another public danger is being reduced by government action in that agreement has been reached with petrol manufacturers to reduce the lead content in petrol. Specifically, the maximum lead levels are being reduced from 0.84g/litre to 0.45g/litre. What this conceals is that the average lead content at the moment is only 0.49g/litre, that by 1976 the average will drop very little, and that this drop will probably be cancelled out by the greater number of vehicles on the road by then. Lead levels are in effect being stabilised, which is better than nothing, but not reduced, despite the recognition of the dangers involved and the more drastic action taken by a number of other countries (Japan, Sweden, Austria, Russia, U.S.A.) and despite the fact that Britain has the greatest density of traffic. Health dangers may also be involved with sulphur and nitrogen oxides, carbon monoxide and a number of other dangerous pollutants neither seen nor smelled.

26. Existing legislation could simply reflect the fact that no one group has a monopoly of power. If so, this need not deny our existing model since the compromise effected is always within a narrow range.

27. Thus, for example, spokesmen of the Department of the Environment counter accusations that government is not adequately controlling pollution, by pointing out the increased hours of sunshine in London (if nothing else, the 1956 Clean Air Act did drastically reduce household smoke) and the higher penalties under the Deposit of Poisonous Wastes Act 1972—*Telegraph* 23.12.72—but without mentioning the numerous similarly dangerous pollutants for which no statutory maximum exists. The very formation of a Department of the Environment suggests a new 'concerned' government image—an image that has not so far been substantiated in action (see for example R. Kimber and J. J. Richardson "The Deposit of Poisonous Wastes Act (1972): a case of government by reaction." Paper given to Young Members Group of the Society of Public Teachers of Law Conference, Sheffield University, 1 September 1973).

28. These are the Conservatives' concern with profit, Labour's concern with jobs (but no imaginative alternative job creation programme) and their common interests in increased economic growth and expansion.

BIBLIOGRAPHY

AKERS, R. L., 'Problems in the sociology of deviance: social definitions and behaviour' *Social Forces* **46**, (1968) pp. 455-65.

ANDERSON, P. and BLACKBURN, R. (eds.), *Towards Socialism* Cornell University Press (1966).

BARR, J., *The Environmental Handbook* London, Ballantine Books (1970).

BECKER, H. S., *Outsiders: Studies in the Sociology of Deviance* New York, Free Press (1963).

BECKER, H. S. (ed.), *Social Problems: A Modern Approach* New York, John Wiley (1966).

BLACKBURN, R., 'The New Capitalism' in Anderson and Blackburn (eds.) op. cit.

BOTTOMORE, T. D., *Elites and Society* London, C. A. Watts & Co. (1964).

BOTTOMORE, T. D., *Classes in Modern Society* London, George Allen and Unwin (1965).

BRAY, J., *The Politics of the Environment* London, Fabian Society (1972).

British Society for Social Responsibility in Science, *The Environment—A Radical Agenda* Nottingham, Russell Press (1972).

BRYCE-SMITH, D., 'Fresh Poison Delivered Daily' *Observer Magazine* (June 1972).

BUGLER, J., *Polluting Britain* Harmondsworth, Penguin (1972).

BURNHAM, J., *The Managerial Revolution* Harmondsworth, Penguin (1945).

CALDWELL, L., 'Authority and Responsibility in Environmental Administration' *Annals American Academy of Political and Social Sciences* (1970), pp. 387-92.

CARSON, W. G., 'White Collar Crime and the Enforcement of Factory Legislation' *British Journal of Criminology* **10** (1970).

CARSON, W. G., Unpublished paper delivered at the 1971 Conference of the British Sociological Association (1970).

CHAMBLISS, W. J., *Crime and the Legal Process* New York, McGraw Hill (1969).

CHAMBLISS, W. J. and SEIDMAN, B., *Law, Order and Power* New York, Addison-Wesley (1971).

COHEN, A. K., *Deviance and Control* Englewood Cliffs N.J., Prentice-Hall (1966).

Conservation Society Manifesto (1971).

DAHRENDORF, R., *Class and Class Conflict in an Industrial Society* London, Routledge and Kegan Paul (1959).

DAVIES, J. C., *The Politics of Pollution* New York, Pegasus (1970).

DICKSON, D. J., 'Bureaucracy and morality: an organisational perspective on a moral crusade' *Social Problems* **16 (2)** (1968) pp. 143-56.

DOUGLAS, J. D., *The Relevance of Sociology* New York, Appleton, Century-Crofts (1970).

DURKHEIM, E., *The Division of Labour in Society* New York, Free Press (1969).

Ecologist, The, Vols. **1**, **2** and **3** (1970–1973).

EHRLICH, P., Interview *Playboy Magazine* (1970).

EHRLICH, P. and HARRIMAN, L., *How to be a Survivor* London, Ballantine (1971).

FRIEDMANN, W., *Law in a Changing Society* Second Edition, Harmondsworth, Penguin (1972).

FULLER, R. C. and MYERS, R. C., 'The Natural History of a Social Problem' *American Sociological Review* (1961).

GOULDNER, A., *The Coming Crisis in Western Sociology* London, Heinemann (1971).

GRAHAM, F. Jnr., *Since Silent Spring* London, Hamish Hamilton (1970).

GUSFIELD, J., *Symbolic Crusade: Status Politics and the American Temperance Movement* Urbana, Illinois University Press (1963).

HAGEVIK, G. K., *Decision Making in Air Pollution Control* New York, Praeger (1970).

HALL, J., *General Principles of Criminal Law* Second Edition, New York, Bobbs-Merrill (1960).

HORTON, J., 'Order and Conflict Theories of Social Problems as Conflicting Ideologies' *American Journal of Sociology* **71** (1966).

JACCOBY, N. H. and PENNANCE, F. G., 'The Polluters, Industry or Government?' *Occasional Paper 36* London Institute of Economic Affairs (1972).

KOLKO, G. (1971), 'Power and Capitalism in Twentieth Century America' in Colfax J. D. and Roach J. L. (eds.) *Radical Sociology,* New York, Basic Books (1971).

LEMERT, E., *Human Deviance, Social Problems and Social Control* Englewood Cliffs N. J., Prentice-Hall (1972).

McLOUGHLIN, J., *The Law Relating to Pollution* Manchester University Press (1972).

MILIBAND, R., *The State in Capitalist Society* London, Merlin Press (1969).

MILLS, C. W., *The Power Elite* Oxford University Press (1956).

NICHOLSON, M., *The Environmental Revolution* London, Hodder & Stoughton (1970).

OPPENHEIM and MILLER, 'Environmental Problems and Legislative Responses'. *Annals American Academy of Political and Social Science* (1970), pp. 387-92.

PEARCE, D., 'Is Ecology Elitist?' *Ecologist* Vol. **3** No. **2** (1973).

PEARCE, F., 'Crime, Corporations and the American Social Order' in Taylor, J. and Taylor L. (eds.) *Politics and Deviance* Harmondsworth, Penguin (1973).

PLATT, J., 'What shall we do?' *Science* Vol **166** (1969).

Pollution: Nuisance or Nemesis? Dept. of Environment London, H.M.S.O. (1972).

The Protection of the Environment; the Fight against Pollution P. Pam 714-4 London, H.M.S.O. 4373 (1970).

QUINNEY, R., 'Crime in Political Perspective' *American Behavioural Scientist* (1966).

QUINNEY, R. (ed.), *The Problem of Crime* New York, Dodd, Mead and Co. (1970).

Rio Tinto Zinc Anti-Report Counter Information Services (1972).

Robens Report *Safety and Health at Work* (Report of the Committee) London, H.M.S.O. (1972).

Royal Commission on Environmental Pollution *First Report* London, H.M.S.O. C.M.N.D. 4585 (1972).

Royal Commission on Environmental Pollution *Second Report* London, H.M.S.O. C.M.N.D. 4894 (1972b).

SANDERSON, J. B., 'The National Smoke Abatement Society and the Clean Air Act' *Political Studies* **9-10** (1956), pp. 1961-2.

SCHUR, E., *Law and Society: A Sociological View* New York, Random House (1968).

SCHWENDINGERS, THE, *Issues in Criminology*. Vol. **5** No. **2** (1970).

TAYLOR, G. R., *The Doomsday Book* London, Thames and Hudson (1970).

TAYLOR, I., WALTON, P. and YOUNG, J., *The New Criminology* London, Routledge & Kegan Paul (1973).

VOLD, G. B., *Theoretical Criminology* Oxford University Press (1958).

WESTERGAARD, J., 'The Withering Away of Class: A Contemporary Myth' in *Anderson and Blackburn* (eds.) op. cit.

Which? Magazine Consumer Association (1973).

YOUNG, J., *The Drugtakers* London, Paladin (1971).

INDEX

Akers, R. C., 10.
Alkali Inspectorate Bill (1973), 62–3.
Alkali Inspectorate, 42, 49, 50, 62–3, 65–73, 83, 87.
Alphacell v. Woodward, 73.
America *see* United States.
American Acadamy for the Advancement of Science, 37.
American Capitalism, 79.
American Politics, 75–80.
Atomic Energy Authority, 57.
Austin, 15.
Automobile Industry, 50, 79.
Ball and Friedman, 73.
Beaver Committee, 59, 60.
Becker, H. S., 24, 26.
Blackburn, R., 45.
'Blueprint for Survival', 35, 59.
Bottomore, T. D., 22, 23, 29.
British Society for Social Responsibility in Science, 81.
Bryce–Smith, D., 83.
Bugler, J., 67, 69, 70, 73.
Burnham, J., 43–4.
Caldwell, L. K., 50, 63.
Cancer, 11.
Capitalism 21, 22, 39, 43–5, 70–72, 83–5.
   Financial 21, 77, 78, 82.
   Post capitalist society, 22.
Capitalist
   Class 38, 43, 85, 86.
   Market economy 35, 39, 80.
Carson, R., 30, 32.
Carson, W. G., 20–1, 29, 49.
Chambliss, W. J., 20, 29.
Chambliss, W. J., and Seidman, B., 18–19, 21, 28, 29, 88.
Class
   Politics, 23, 26, 38.
   Social, 21–2.
   Ruling, 23.
Clean Air Act 1956, 32, 42, 51, 61, 72, 82, 83.
Clean Air Act 1968, 43, 52.
Clean Air Bill 1956, 59, 61.
Cohen, A. K., 16.

Confederation of British Industries, 47.
Conservation Society, 31, 81.
Conservative Party, 83, 84, 90.
Crosland, C. A. R., 53.
Dahrendorf, R., 22, 29.
Davies, J. C., 37, 41, 42, 55, 57, 63, 66.
D.D.T., 48.
Deposit of Poisonous Wastes Act, 1972, 89.
Dixon, D. J., 25, 39.
Durkheim, E., 14, 16, 17–18.
Ecology, 32.
Ecological movement, 30.
Ecologist magazine, 35, 40, 41, 48, 81.
Ehrlich, P., 31, 32, 80.
Environmental Consciousness, 30–34
Environmental lobby, 46, 81.
Evelyn, J., 31, 34.
Expressive politics, 26, 36, 78, 81.
Federation of British Industries, 60.
Friends of the Earth, 31, 81.
Friedmann, W., 10, 11, 16, 17, 19, 53.
Fuller and Myers, 23, 29.
Gouldner, A., 36, 41, 81, 86.
Government, 39, 55, 59, 60, 77, 78, 79, 81, 85, 86.
Government agencies, 57.
Graham, F. Jnr., 39, 41.
Gusfield, J., 25, 26, 29.
Hall, J., 20, 29.
Hagevik, G. K., 55, 63.
Horton, J., 11.
House of Representatives, 57.
Image management, 48, 58, 71.
Imperial Smelting Corporation, 68.
Industry, 22, 39, 42–53, 55, 56, 57, 58, 59, 60, 61, 65, 69–72, 77, 78, 79, 81.
Industrial Conflict, 22.
Interest groups, 20, 21, 25–26, 27, 31, 33, 36–41, 55, 56, 57, 75, Chapter VII.
Interest group theory, 16–21.